Arduino Programming

A Comprehensive Beginner's Tutorial to Master
Arduino Programming Sequentially

Ryan roffe

TABLE OF CONTENTS

Introduction to Arduino

In case you've never heard of an Arduino before, it is an open-source electronic interface that has two parts: the first is the programable circuit board, and the other is a coding program of your choice to run to your computer. Arduinos come in many forms, including the Arduino Uno, LilyPad Arduino, Redboard, Arduino Mega, Arduino Leonardo, and others which we will explain later on.

If you're unfamiliar with programming, this is a good place to start. The Arduino can be programmed in various types of programming languages, and its wide array of Arduino options can give you more programming experience. Arduinos come with additional attachments, some in the form of sensors, and others can be obtained anywhere and can be attached to the various ports on an Arduino. Arduino is a great stepping stone on the way to understanding programming and sensor interaction.

In programming languages, there is always the well-known program, "Hello World" that is showcased on the screen. In the microcontroller world that we are in, this phase or first program is indicated by a blinking of the light, "on" and "off" to show that everything you have set up works correctly.

We will look at the sketches in their entirety and explain the details after explaining the code. If you go through something that you cannot make something out of, keep on reading, and it will be clear.

Let us look at this program, to show you how we will be breaking down the codes.

Const int PinkL = 13;

Void setup ()

{ pinMode (PinkL, OUTPUT); }

Void loop ()

{ digitalWrite(PinkL, HIGH);

delay (600);

digitalWrite(PinkL, LOW);

delay(600);}

On the first part

Const int PinkL = 13;

This line is used to define a constant that is used throughout the program to specify a particular value. All pins are recommended to have this because it makes it easy for software change if the circuit is still the same. In programming in Arduino, the constants are commonly named starting with the letter "k".

The second to part

Void setup ()

{pinMode (PinkL, OUTPUT);}

The OUTPUT is pin 13. This now makes Arduino control the coding to the pins, instead of reading from it.

The third part

Void loop()

{digitalWrite (PinkL, HIGH);

delay(600);

digitalWrite(PinkL, LOW);

Delay(600);}

This is where the core part of the code is. A HIGH is written to the pin that leads to the turning of the LED. When you place HIGH, it means that 5V is the pin's output. The other option we have is LOW, which means that you are putting 0V out.

A delay() is called to delay the number of milliseconds that is sent to it. Since we send 600, there will be a delay of 0.6 of a second. The LED goes off, and this is attributed to the LOW that is written as an output on the pin.

A 600 milliseconds delay will be activated.

This will be the sequence until the Arduino goes off or the power is disconnected from it.

Before you start digesting more content, try this program out and ensure that it works just fine. To test if you have set your LED in reverse order, the following might happen. On the UNO board, you have pin 13 connected to a Light Emitting Diode connected. When it blinks and the breadboard LED does not blink, then you might have connected your LED in reverse. In case you see that it is blinking once in a second, then the program has not been sent to the Arduino successfully.

When you've completed the programming, place comments in the coding lines to instruct the Arduino. These comments can instruct your Arduino to blink the LED intermittently or through various sequences.

The programs we normally write are usually meant for the computers and not for people to understand once they are opened up. There is a good provision that allows us, humans, to read the program easily and the computer will have no clue about it. There are two comments that are possible in this program:

1. The block comment style starts with two characters, /* which progresses until */ is seen. Multiple lines are then crossed and here are a few examples.

/* This is the first line*/

/* the program was successful*/

/* we

*are

*going

far/

2. Commenting can be done on a line that has the backslash operator //. This is the part that is meant for humans and not machines. It is another way to insert a comment.

When you add comments in a program, you will have a code that looks like the statement above.

You will find in the following pages, that if there is no number next to the line of code, it indicates a comment continuation from the line at the top. We might not showcase this in perfection because we are using a limited space in our book. You will find a hyphen at the line's end that is continued and a hyphen along the continuation line. This is just our way of handling it, but in an IDE, you won't find it and you need not type them.

/*

* Program Name: Blink123

*Author: James Aden

* Date written: 24 July 2017

*Description:

* Turns an LED on for a sixth-hundred of a second, then for another sixth-hundred of a- -second on a continuous repetitive session

*/

/* Pin Definitions */

Const int PinkL = 13;

/*

*Functions Name: setup

*Purpose: Run once after system power up

*/

Void setup(){pinMode(PinkL,OUTPUT);}

/*

Void
loop(){digitalWrite(PinkL,HIGH);Delay(600);digitalWrite(PinkL,LOW);Delay(600):}

Gotchas

If you find out that your program does not compile, or it gives you a different result than what you need, here are a few things that people get confused about:

The programming language is normally sensitive to capitalization of letters. For instance, myVar is considered different to MyVar.

Tabs, blank lines, and white spaces are equivalent to a single space, making it easier for one to read.

Code blocks are normally grouped using curly braces, i.e., "{" and "}"

All open parenthesis have a corresponding closing parenthesis, i.e. "(" and ")"

Numbers don't have commas. So instead of writing 1,000, ensure that you write 1000.

All program statements MUST end with a semicolon. This means that each statement except for the following two cases:

-In comments

- after curly braces are placed "}"

Assignment task to test what you have learned:
1. Alter the delay time of your LED before it comes back on to stick to 1.5 seconds. Leave the ON time of the LED limited to 600 milliseconds.

2. From pin 13, change to pin 2, making it the new connection to the LED. Keep in mind that both the circuit & and the program will be different.

This is just a basis for basic Arduino programming. In the rest of the book, we will be looking at how Arduinos can be programmed with respect to different functions. If you're new to programming, don't let the above codes frighten you. Coding takes practice, but it relatively easy to learn, just like a new language.

CHAPTER 1: What is Arduino?

With the age of technology being in full swing, there is an increase in the average person's technological literacy. More and more people are becoming versed in the hardware and software of the modern age, whether as a dabbling hobbyist or as a professional engineer.

For whatever reason, you and many others have been attracted to Arduino. Perhaps you have seen the variety of projects online or in-person that are built on Arduino technologies, or maybe you have heard of the flexibility and ease of building gadgets with Arduino. Whatever the case, you are interested in learning more about Arduino and how to utilize the technology in your own life. First, let us look at what Arduino is and its history.

History of Arduino

The Arduino technology started as an idea in 2003 by Hernando Barragán to simplify the BASIC stamp microcontroller and reduce costs for non-engineering students to purchase such technology at the Interactive Design Institute in Ivrea, Italy. A microcontroller is a small computer board that can be programmed to perform certain functions. At the time, BASIC stamp microcontrollers cost $100 and upward, and, as we will see later, Arduino certainly reduced the costs while maintaining the ability to perform various functions and the ease of programming such functions.

Supervised by Massimo Banzi and Casey Reas, Barragán worked in the computer language called Processing to create the environment, IDE (Arduino's official coding environment and program). He fiddled with the Wiring platform technology to come up with the hardware called ATmega168, the first Arduino microcontroller.

Later in 2003, Massimo Banzi, David Mellis, and David Cuartielles added support for Wiring to their microcontroller board, named ATmega8, and they reworked the Wiring source code, naming it Arduino. Together, the three along with Tom Igoe and Gianluca Martino continued to develop Arduino technologies, and by the year 2013, 700,000 microcontroller boards were sold from the New York City supplier, Adafruit Industries, alone.

After some issues with establishing the trademark for Arduino, which resulted in a split in the company for a few years, Arduino is now a single company that is committed to the development of hardware and software usable by the average person or hobbyist, but also flexible enough to be of interest to the professional engineer.

But what *is* Arduino?

This history of Arduino might sound as convoluted as the technology itself seems to you. Full of many puzzling and confusing elements, you might feel overwhelmed by the language of "microcontrollers," "environments," and "languages." However, this book is intended to demystify Arduino. We will start here, beginning with the definition of Arduino.

How it works is as follows: one purchases the hardware that is appropriate to his or her purposes and then, on a more powerful Windows, Macintosh OSX, or Linux computer, and codes or write instructions for the board and uploads the instructions via a cable. The code is then stored on the microcontroller, and it functions according to the instructions, such as activating a beeping sound when light filters in through an opening door. The light activates a sensor connected to the microcontroller, like an alarm.

Who Uses Arduino?

A wide array of people uses Arduino for various projects and hobbies, as well as for professional uses. It is known for being simple and straightforward enough for beginners, deep and rich enough for the beginner to grow, and with enough potential for a more advanced user to utilize.

Teachers and students use Arduino, and indeed are the intended consumer base for the products, as Arduino offers a low-cost way to build scientific instruments. This allows teachers and students to practice and demonstrate chemistry and physics principles, as well as get started with programming and building robots.

Designers and architects might use Arduino technologies to build interactive models and prototypes of what they hope to develop on a full-scale. Musicians and artists also use Arduino microcontrollers to experiment with new instruments or techniques in their art.

Just about anyone can use Arduino, including children, that want to start tinkering with coding and computer hardware, as well as hobbyists who simply want to learn a bit about software and microcomputers.

CHAPTER 2: The 6 Advantages of Arduino

- The driving force behind creating Arduino microcontrollers was cost-efficiency. Rather than the $100 that some other boards cost, a pre-assembled Arduino board costs less than $50, and the boards that can be manually put together cost even less.

- The Arduino environment, IDE, works across different platforms. This means that you can use a Windows computer like any other microcontroller board would probably require, but you can also use a Macintosh OSX computer, or a computer running Linux and work just as easily with the Arduino software. This opens up the use of microcontrollers to the Apple user and the open-source Linux user.

- The software for Arduino is open-source. The tools, or strings of code that you use to instruct the microcontroller to accomplish certain functions, are accessible by anyone. You do not have to purchase a license to use these tools so that teachers can teach students about them and students can learn them without added cost.

- The open-source tools are also extendable by the C++ libraries and the AVR-C coding language, meaning that those with more in-depth knowledge of code would be able to benefit from using these technologies as well. There is depth to the software and programming features that allow the more dedicated person to go deeper while being enough of a straightforward coding language to allow the hobbyist to tinker as well.

- The environment in which a person codes for the microcontroller is simple and clear. This means that the computer program, IDE, which you would use to program the instructions for the microcontroller, is straightforward and easy to understand. This makes working with the software a smooth experience.

- The open-source hardware. Arduino board technologies are published under a Creative Commons license. Anyone who desires and has the knowledge to do so could find and create their own hardware to use with Arduino software programming in the IDE environment. Even those who are not experienced circuit designers can use a breadboard to create their own Arduino circuit-board.

CHAPTER 3: Key Terms in Understanding Arduino

When working with Arduino technologies, it is helpful to understand the terminology of Arduino. You will need to understand the terminology to choose a board, write the coded instructions, set up the microcontroller for use, and finally using the Arduino board. In this chapter, you will find some key terms that will aid you greatly in your endeavor to become an Arduino user.

As mentioned earlier, Arduino is open-source, meaning you can use it and teach it to others without violating any copyright laws. It is based on easy-to-use hardware, which is the actual physical computer board with which you will be working, and straightforward software, the coded instructions with which you will use to direct the hardware to perform a task of your choosing. The software is also known as code, and the individual pieces of instructions are called tools.

Anatomy of the Arduino Board

The board itself contains a good number of parts. The digital pins run along the edges of most Arduino microcontrollers and are used for input, or sensing of a condition, and output, the response that the controller makes to the input. For example, the input might be that the light sensor senses darkness, that is, a lack of light. It will then close a circuit lighting up a bulb as output: a nightlight for your child.

On most boards, there will be a Pin LED, associated with a specific pin, like Pin 13 on the Arduino Uno. This Pin LED is the only output possibility built into the board, and it will help you with your first project of a "blink sketch," which will be explained later. The Pin LED is also used for debugging or fixing the code you have written so that it has no mistakes in it. The Power LED is what its name implies: it lights up when the board is receiving power or is "turned on." This can also be helpful in debugging your code.

There exists on every board the microcontroller itself, called the ATmega microcontroller, which is the brain of the entire board. It receives your instructions and acts accordingly. Without this, the entire board would have no functionality.

Analog in pins exist on the opposite edge of the board from the digital pins on the Arduino Uno. It is an input into the Arduino system. Analog means that the signal which is input is not constant but instead varies with time, such as audio input. In the example of audio input, the auditory input in a room varies with the people in the room talking and with the noises filtering in from outside the room.

GND and 5V pins are used to create additional power of 5V to the circuit and microcontroller. The power connector is most often on the edge of the Arduino board, and it is used to provide power to the microcontroller when it is not plugged into the USB. The USB port can be used as a power source as well, but its main function is to upload, or transfer, your sketch, or set of instructions that you have coded, from your computer to the Arduino.

TX and RX LED's are used to indicate that there is a transfer of information occurring. This indication of communication will happen when you upload your sketches from your computer to the Arduino so that they will blink rapidly during the exchange.

The reset button is as it sounds: it resets the microcontroller to factory settings and erases any information you have uploaded to the Arduino.

Other Terms about Working with Arduino

There are three types of memory in an Arduino system. Memory is the space where information is stored.

Flash memory is where the code for the program that you have written is stored. It is also called the "program space," because it is used for the program automatically when you upload it to the Arduino. This type of memory remains intact when the power is cut off, or when the Arduino is turned off.

SRAM (static random-access memory) is the space used by the sketch or program you have created to create, store, and work with information from the input sources to create an output. This type of storage disappears once the power is turned off.

EEPROM is like a tiny a hard-drive that allows the programmer to store information other than the program itself when the Arduino is turned off. There are separate instructions for the EEPROM, for reading, writing, and erasing, as well as other functions.

Certain digital pins will be designated as PWM pins, meaning that they can create analog using digital means. Analog, as we remember, means that input (or output) is varied and not constant. Normally, digital pins can only create a constant flow of energy. However, PWM pins can vary the "pulse" of energy between 0 and 5 Volts. Certain tasks that you program can only be carried out by PWM pins.

In addition, in comparing microcontroller boards, you will want to look at clock speed, which is the speed at which the microcontroller operates. The faster the speed, the more responsive it the board will be, but the more battery or energy it will consume as well.

UART measures the number of serial communication lines the device can handle. Serial communication lines are lines that transfer data serially, that is, in a line rather than in parallel or simultaneously. It requires much less hardware to process things serially than in parallel.

Some projects will have you connecting devices to the Internet of Things, which essentially describes the interconnectedness of devices, other than desktop and laptop computers, to various networks in order to share information. Everything from smart refrigerators, to smartphones, to smart TV's are connected to the Internet of Things.

CHAPTER 4: Understanding the Choices

Now that we know some basics in understanding the Arduino microcontroller boards let us look at the various options you have when purchasing an Arduino board. We will look at price, functionality, amount of memory, and other features to help make your decision as easy and straightforward as possible.

Uno

This is the board in which most people start their Arduino journey. It is on the smaller side in terms of memory but is very flexible in functionality and a great tool for beginners and those wanting to try their hand and mind at Arduino. This model has a mini-USB port which allows you to upload directly to the board without using a breakout board or other extra hardware.

Price: $24.95

Flash Memory: 32kB

SRAM: 2kB

EEPROM: 1kB

Processing Speed: 16MHz

Digital Pins: 14 pins

PWM Pins: 6 pins

Analog In: 6 pins

Operating Power: 5V

Input Power: 7-12V

Leonardo

The Leonardo microcontroller board is functional out-of-the-box: all you need is a micro-USB cable and a computer to get started. In addition, the computer can recognize the Leonardo as a mouse or a keyboard due to its ATmega32U4 processor.

Price: $19.80

Flash Memory: 32kB

SRAM: 2.5kB

EEPROM: 1kB

Processing Speed: 16MHz

Digital Pins: 20 pins

PWM Pins: 7 pins

Analog In: 12 pins

Operating Power: 5V

Input Power: 7-12V

101

This microcontroller contains a lot of features that are not available in other beginner models. For example, you can connect to the board through Bluetooth Low Energy connectivity from your phone. In addition, it comes with an accelerometer and a gyroscope built in to recognize motion in all directions with its six-axis sensitivity. It can recognize gestures as well.

Put together, these features allow you to have motion of or around the device be the input to which the microcontroller will respond with an output.

Price: $30.00

Flash Memory: 196kB

SRAM: 24kB

EEPROM: 0kB

Processing Speed: 32MHz

Digital Pins: 14 pins

PWM Pins: 4 pins

Analog In: 6 pins

Operating Power: 3.3V

Input Power: 7-12V

Esplora

This board is based on the Leonardo but comes with even more technology built into it so that you do not have to learn as much electronics to get up and running. Instead, you can learn as you see the processes work themselves out.

The input sensors that are built in include a joystick, a slider, a temperature sensor, a microphone, an accelerometer, and a light sensor. It also includes some sound and light outputs. It can expand its capabilities by attaching to other technology called a TFT LCD screen through two Tinker kit input/output connections.

Price: $43.89

Flash Memory: 32kB

SRAM: 2.5kB

EEPROM: 1kB

Processing Speed: 16MHz

Digital Pins: n/a

PWM Pins: n/a

Analog In: n/a

Operating Power: 5V

Input Power: 7-12V

Mega 2560

This microcontroller is designed for larger projects like robotics and 3D printers. It has many times the number of digital pins and analog in pins, as well as almost three times the number of PWM pins. This, along with the many times multiplied flash storage, SRAM, and EEPROM allows for projects that require more instructions. There is space for greater complexity and specificity in this Arduino board.

Price: $45.95

Flash Memory: 256kB

SRAM: 8kB

EEPROM: 4kB

Processing Speed: 16MHz

Digital Pins: 54 pins

PWM Pins: 15 pins

Analog In: 16 pins

Operating Power: 5V

Input Power: 7-12V

UART: 4 lines

Zero

This is an extension of the Arduino Uno technologies that were developed. It is a 32-bit extension of Uno, and it increases performance with a vastly increased processing speed, 16 times the amount of SRAM and a many times multiplied flash memory. You will pay for the extensions, at almost twice the price of the Uno, but you much more than double your capabilities with this hardware.

One other advantage of the Zero is that it has a built-in feature called Atmel's Embedded Debugger, abbreviated as EDBG, which helps you debug your code without using extra hardware and thereby increases your efficiency in the software coding.

Price: $42.90

Flash Memory: 256kB

SRAM: 32kB

EEPROM: n/a

Processing Speed: 48MHz

Digital Pins: 14 pins

PWM Pins: 10 pins

Analog In: 6 pins

Analog Out: 1 pin

Operating Power: 3.3V

Input Power: 7-12V

UART: 2 lines

USB port: 2 micro-USB ports

Due

This is a novelty in the microcontroller board world because it is built on a 32-bit ARM core microcontroller, giving it a great deal of power and functionality. It has an extremely quick processor and 4 UART's, giving it a lot of flexibility and availability to perform multiple functions. It is used for larger scale Arduino projects, and while it might not be your first board, you would do well to consider it for any bigger projects you have down the line.

Price: $37.40

Flash Memory: 512kB

SRAM: 96kB

EEPROM: n/a

Processing Speed: 84MHz

Digital Pins: 54 pins

PWM Pins: 12 pins

Analog In: 12 pins

Analog Out: 2 pins

Operating Power: 3.3V

Input Power: 7-12V

UART: 4 lines

USB ports: 2 micro-USB ports

Mega ADK

This is based on the Mega2560 Arduino board, with incredible memory capacity and a lot of availability for input and output. The difference between the Mega2560 and the Mega ADK is that the Mega ADK is compatible specifically with Android technologies, such as Samsung phones and tablets, Asus technologies, and other non-iOS, non-Windows, mobile devices that use Android. It comes at a hefty almost $50 price tag, but if you are looking to incorporate Android into your project, this would be the board with which you would want to do so.

Price: $47.30

Flash Memory: 256kB

SRAM: 8kB

EEPROM: 4kB

Processing Speed: 16MHz

Digital Pins: 54 pins

PWM Pins: 15 pins

Analog In: 16 pins

Operating Power: 5V

Input Power: 7-12V

UART: 4 lines

Arduino Pro (8 MHz)

This is the SparkFun company's take on the ATmega328 board. It is basically the Uno for professionals and is meant to be semi-permanent in installation of an object or technology. The 8MHz version is less powerful than the Uno by half, but it is also a good deal cheaper. It requires more knowledge of hardware to get this one working, as it does not have a USB port or a way to power the board by USB, and thus must have a connection to an FTDI cable or breakout board to communicate with the board and upload sketches. Once you get through the technicalities of getting this board hooked up to your computer, however, it functions like a half-power Uno. Unlike the 16MHz Arduino Pro, this 8MHz Pro can be powered by a lithium battery.

Price: $14.95

Flash Memory: 16kB

SRAM: 1kB

EEPROM: 0.512kB

Processing Speed: 8MHz

Digital Pins: 14 pins

PWM Pins: 6 pins

Analog In: 6 pins

Operating Power: 3.3V

Input Power: 3.35-12V

UART: 1 line

Arduino Pro (16 MHz)

This is the 16MHz version of the Arduino Pro by SparkFun. It is the same amount of power as the Uno but has the same drawbacks as the 8MHz Pro: you will need to find an FTDI cable or purchase a breakout board from SparkFun in order to make the board compatible with your computer to upload sketches. This means learning a *bit* more about the technology than if you were to start with the Uno, but after getting things set up, this will function the same as the Uno.

Price: $14.95

Flash Memory: 32kB

SRAM: 2kB

EEPROM: 1kB

Processing Speed: 16MHz

Digital Pins: 14 pins

PWM Pins: 6 pins

Analog In: 6 pins

Operating Power: 5V

Input Power: 5-12V

UART: 1 line

Arduino M0

This board is an extension of Arduino Uno, giving the Uno the 32-bit power of an ARM Cortex M0 core. This will not be your first board, but it might be your most exciting project. It will allow a creative mind to develop wearable technology, make objects with high tech automation, create yet-unseen robotics, come up with new ideas for the Internet of Things, or many other fantastic projects. This is a powerful extension of the straightforward technology of the Uno, and thus it has the flexibility to become almost anything you could imagine.

Price: $22.00

Flash Memory: 256 kB

SRAM: 32kB

Processing Speed: 48MHz

Digital Pins: 20 pins

PWM Pins: 12 pins

Analog In: 6 pins

Operating Power: 3.3V

Input Power: 5-15V

Arduino M0 Pro

This is the same extended technology of the Uno as the Arduino M0, but it has the added functionality and capability of debugging its own software with the Atmel's Embedded Debugger (EDBG) integrated into the board itself. This creates an interface with the board in which you can debug, or, in other words, a way to interact with the board where you can find the problems in the code you have provided and fix the issues.

Price: $42.90

Flash Memory: 256 kB

SRAM: 32kB

Processing Speed: 48MHz

Digital Pins: 20 pins

PWM Pins: 12 pins

Analog In: 6 pins

Operating Power: 3.3V

Input Power: 5-15V

Arduino YÚN (based on ATmega32U4)

The Arduino YÚN is a great board to use when connecting to the Internet of Things. It is perfect for if you want to design a device connected to a network, like the Internet or a data network. It has built-in ethernet support, which would give you a wired connection to a network, and Wi-Fi capabilities, allowing you to connect cordlessly to the Internet. The YÚN has a processor that supports Linux code in the operating system, or code language, of Linino OS. This gives it extra power and capabilities but retains the ease of use of Arduino.

Price: $68.20

Flash Memory: 32kB

SRAM: 2.5kB

EEPROM: 1kB

Processing Speed: 16MHz

Digital Pins: 20 pins

PWM Pins: 7 pins

Analog In: 12 pins

Operating Power: 5V

UART: 1 line

Arduino Ethernet

This Arduino board is based on the ATmega328, the same microcontroller as the Arduino Uno. Pins 10 through 13 are reserved for interacting with Ethernet, and as such, this board has less input/output capability than the Uno and other Arduino microcontroller boards. It does not connect via USB, but rather through the Ethernet cord, which has the option also to power the microcontroller. There exists on this board, unlike other boards, the option to expand storage through a microSD card reader. The method in which you upload your sketches to this board is similar to the Arduino Pro, and that is via an FTDI USB cable or through an FTDI breakout board. This Arduino model is more complex than a lot of the boards at which we have taken a look, but it has functionalities that are not possible on other boards as well.

Price: $43.89

Flash Memory: 32kB

SRAM: 2kB

EEPROM: 1kB

Processing Speed: 16MHz

Digital Pins: 14 pins

PWM Pins: 4 pins

Analog In: 6 pins

Operating Power: 5V

Input Power: 7-12V

Arduino Tian

The Tian is a miniature computer, with a built-in microprocessor on top of the microcontroller. It has Wi-Fi capabilities like the Arduino YÚN as well as the ethernet capabilities of the YÚN and the Ethernet models. You pay a costly price for the increased functionality and power, but it is many times worth what you pay. This is a fast processor, at 560 MHz clock speed, and on top of it all, this has Bluetooth capabilities. This board also uses the Linino OS, based on the Linux operating system and on OpenWRT.

Price: $95.70

Flash Memory: 256kB (+16MB flash from the microprocessor + 4GB eMMC from the microprocessor)

SRAM: 32kB (+64MB DDR2 RAM from microprocessor)

Processing Speed: 48MHz (560 MHz on the microprocessor)

Digital Pins: 20 pins

Analog In: 6 pins

Operating Power: 3.3V

Input Power: 5V

Industrial 101

The Industrial 101 is essentially a small, less capable YÚN for a little more than half the price. It is intended for "product integration," or, in other words, is meant to be used in long-standing projects. It is intended to function in a semi-permanent role within whatever you are building. The board has built-in Wi-Fi capabilities, a USB connection port, and one Ethernet port by which you can connect to networks via Ethernet cord. This board can be connected to your computer via micro-USB in order to upload your sketches for programming.

Price: $38.50

Flash Memory: 16MB on the processor

SRAM: 2.5KB (RAM is 64 MB DDR2 on the processor)

EEPROM: 1kB

Processing Speed: 16MHz (400MHz for the processor)

Digital Pins: 20 pins

PWM Pins: 7 pins

Analog In: 12 pins

Operating Power: 3.3V

Input Power: 5V

Arduino Leonardo ETH

This is the Arduino Leonardo microcontroller board with an Ethernet port to allow the project to extend to the Internet of Things. You can use the Internet to control the sensors in this way, using your own device as a server or signal provider, or as a client, communicating with the microcontroller to receive instructions. This also contains a micro-USB connector to upload your sketches to the flash memory on the Leonardo ETH. This eliminates the need for a breakout board or TKDI cable. Like the Ethernet model of Arduino, this has the option to be powered by the Ethernet cable as well. There is an onboard microSD card reader for extra storage as well. Essentially, this is a powered-up Leonardo, with greater flexibility to be used in a wider variety of projects and the capacity to be connected to the Internet of Things.

Price: $43.89

Flash Memory: 32kB (4kB is used by the bootloader, so only 28K available for use)

SRAM: 2.5kB

Processing Speed: 16MHz

Digital Pins: 20 pins

PWM Pins: 7 pins

Analog In: 12 pins

Operating Power: 5V

Input Power: 7-12V

Gemma

This Arduino is made by Adafruit Technologies in the USA. The Arduino Gemma is a miniature microcontroller board that is intended to be worn. It indeed has less space and room for functionality than the non-wearable boards, but for many wearable projects, you will not need the robustness of some of the other Arduino microcontroller boards. There is a micro-USB connection on this board, so you do not need a breakout board or TKDI cable. Instead, you simply upload a sketch via the micr0-USB connection and then power the microcontroller by micro-USB or by battery connection.

Price: $9.95

Flash Memory: 8kB

SRAM: 0.5kB

EEPROM: 0.5kB

Processing Speed: 8MHz

Digital Pins: 3 pins

PWM Pins: 2 pins

Analog In: 1 pin

Operating Power: 3.3V

Input Power: 4-16V

Lilypad Arduino USB

This board is round and based on the ATmega32u4 Arduino microcontroller. It contains a micro-USB connected for ease of uploading sketches and for powering the board. There is also a JST connection built in so that, should you decide to power the board by battery, you can do so by connecting a 3.7V Lithium Polymer battery. The difference between the Lilypad Arduino USB and the rest of the Lilypad Arduino models is that the

USB model contains the micro-USB port standard, eliminating the need for a breakout board or TKDI adapter. In addition, the board can be seen as a mouse or a keyboard by the computer, among other things.

This board is intended to be worn, like the Gemma. It can be sewn into clothing or otherwise attached to one's body to perform whatever function you have programmed it to perform.

Price: $24.95 (available on SparkFun)

Flash Memory: 32kB

SRAM: 2.5kB

EEPROM: 1kB

Processing Speed: 8MHz

Digital Pins: 9 pins

PWM Pins: 4 pins

Analog In: 4 pins

Operating Power: 3.3V

Input Power: 3.8-5V

Lilypad Arduino Main Board

This is another wearable Arduino microcontroller board. It can be sewn into a piece of fabric or combined with other sensors, actuators, and a power supply to be something you carry with you with the functionality you have programmed yourself. It requires a breakout board and TKDI cable to upload your sketch to the microcontroller's flash memory, but once you have that piece taken care of, you have an inexpensive, wearable device that you have created yourself.

Price: $19.95 (available on SparkFun)

Flash Memory: 16kB (2kB are used by the bootloader so only 14kB are available for use by the programmer)

SRAM: 1kB

EEPROM: 0.512kB

Processing Speed: 8MHz

Digital Pins: 14 pins

PWM Pins: 6 pins

Analog In: 6 pins

Operating Power: 2.7-5.5V

Input Power: 2.7-5.5V

Lilypad Arduino Simple

This Arduino microcontroller board model differs from the Lilypad Arduino Main Board in that it possesses only 9 digital input/output pins, about 2/3 the number of pins on the Main Board. This is a good board for simpler projects that do not require as many inputs and outputs. It is also more powerful than the Main Board, having twice the flash memory, SRAM, and EEPROM. This is a powerful, but less functional version of the Lilypad Arduino Main Board meant to be worn as a transportable device.

Price: $19.95 (available on SparkFun)

Flash Memory: 32kB

SRAM: 2kB

EEPROM: 1kB

Processing Speed: 8MHz

Digital Pins: 9 pins

PWM Pins: 5 pins

Analog In: 4 pins

Operating Power: 2.7-5.5V

Input Power: 2.7-5.5V

Lilypad Arduino Simple Snap

This is a more expensive version of the Lilypad Arduino Simple and is also designed to create wearable devices and e-textiles. It solves an essential problem of the previous versions: washing the textiles in which is it embedded. With the other models of Lilypad Arduino and with the Gemma, one removes the power source and then hand washes the material in which the microcontroller is embedded or sewn. Then, one must wait for the entire circuity to dry before powering back up, or else a short can happen and ruin the technology.

With the Lilypad Arduino Simple Snap, the 9 pins for input/output are snappable buttons such that the microcontroller board can be removed from the material to which it is initially attached. Then, the material can be washed, and the board is returned to its home on the fabric.

The Lilypad Arduino Simple Snap also has a built-in lithium polymer battery (LiPo battery), which can be recharged by attaching power to the charging circuit. The way this board is designed, it has the advantage of being able to detach and attach to a new project.

Price: $29.95 (available on SparkFun)

Flash Memory: 32kB

SRAM: 2kB

EEPROM: 1kB

Processing Speed: 8MHz

Digital Pins: 9 pins

PWM Pins: 5 pins

Analog In: 4 pins

Operating Power: 2.7-5.5V

Input Power: 2.7-5.5V

Other Boards

There exist other boards, like the Arduino Mini, the Pro Mini, the Arduino Robot Control, the Arduino Robot Motor, the Arduino BT, and many others, with the number of options growing quickly.

If you're a beginner, it is recommended that you start with a basic board such as the UNO. Once you're ready for some more advanced projects, these other models might be something you'd like to investigate further! Choosing your Arduino board depends on both the function and convenience of each board. As mentioned above, the UNO is generally considered the board for beginners, but consider how voltage, current, and resistance plays a part in your selections. The inputting power for each project depends on how you will use the board.

For now, let us discover how to get started with Arduino.

CHAPTER 5: Choosing and Setting Up the Arduino

The first step in setting up your Arduino microcontroller will be to choose an Arduino board with which you want to work.

Choosing a Board

When looking at the options for Arduino Boards, there are a few factors you will want to consider before making a choice. Before deciding on a board, ask yourself the following questions:

How much power do I need to run the application I have in mind?

You might not know the exact measure of flash memory and processing power that you require for your project, but there is a clear difference between the functioning of a simple nightlight that changes colors and a robotic hand with many moving parts. The latter would require a more robust Arduino microcontroller board, with faster processing, more flash memory, and more SRAM than the more straightforward night light idea.

How many digital and analog pins will I require to have the functionality that I desire?

Again, you don't need to have an extremely specific idea in mind but knowing whether you need more pins or less will have a great effect on which board you choose. If you are going for a simple first project, you could get away with having less digital, PWM, and analog pins, while if you are looking to do something more complex, you will want to consider the boards with a great number of pins in general.

Do I want this to be a wearable device?

There are a few options for wearable devices so, of course, this question will not entirely make the decision for you. It will, however, help narrow down the choices and steer you in a direction, with Lilypads and the Gemma or other comparable technologies being your best options.

Do I want to connect to the Internet of Things? If so, how?

If you want connectivity to the Internet of Things, your work will be made much easier by the YÚN, the Tian, the Ethernet, the Leonardo ETH, or the Industrial 101. These have the capabilities of Ethernet connection as well as Wi-Fi capability so you will be able to connect to a network like the Internet and share data or interact with and control other devices on the Internet of Things.

Getting Started on Arduino IDE

The Arduino Software runs in an environment called IDE. This means that you will either need to download the desktop IDE to code in or code online on the online IDE.

The first way that you might access IDE, downloading the desktop application, has a few options to suit the various devices that you might be using. First, there is the Windows desktop application. You can also access it from a Windows tablet or Windows phone with the Windows application. Next, there is the Macintosh OSX version, which allows IDE to run on Apple laptops and desktops, but not on Apple mobile devices like iPhones and iPads. Finally, there are three options for running Arduino IDE on Linux: the 32-bit, the 64-bit, and the Linux ARM version. If you prefer this option to the web browser option, you will simply need to visit the Arduino IDE site by heading to https://www.arduino.cc/en/Main/Software

There, you can download the appropriate version of desktop IDE. Next, you will run the installation application, click through the options presented, and you should have a running Arduino IDE environment in just a few minutes.

This allows you to access the IDE software from Android devices and Apple mobile devices as well since it is based in a web browser that runs on its own platform rather than on the Android or iOS platforms. You can also run the web browser on various computer types, including Linux, Microsoft Windows, and Apple Macintosh. This will allow you to upload your sketches to the Cloud, that is, to store the information you have coded in a secure location that you can then re-access from another device by connection to the Internet.

Coding a Program for Your Arduino

Next you will write code for a program that you want the Arduino board to run. We will cover how to write code for the Arduino boards in the next chapter, but for now let us be sure to understand that the code is written in the IDE on the computer, tablet, or phone, in either the desktop application or the web application. This allows you to see the entire code at once, allowing for easier debugging, or removing of errors.

Once you write the code, you will want to run it and troubleshoot or debug any errors that you find. You will best be able to do this by applying the coded program to the Arduino board and seeing if it runs. To do this, you will need to proceed to the next step of uploading your sketch.

Connecting to the Arduino Board

Some of the boards come with built-in USB, mini-USB, or micro-USB ports. Examples would be the Uno and the Leonardo, for the more beginning stages of your Arduino career. Simply insert the appropriate end of the USB cord into your computer and the other end into the particular USB port that is present on the board you possess, and the Arduino IDE software should recognize the type of board it is. If it does not, you can always choose the correct board from a dropdown menu.

Sometimes you will need to use a TKDI cable or a breakout board in order to make the Arduino compatible with your computer. This means you will insert the TKDI into the TKDI port on the Arduino microcontroller board and then connect it either to your computer or to another board. If you connect the TKDI cable to a breakout board, you will do as you did with the USB-compatible boards: insert the appropriate end of the cord to the breakout board and the other end to the computer. Again, the computer's Arduino IDE software program should recognize your Arduino board, but you can always choose from a dropdown menu should it fail to recognize it.

Uploading to the Arduino Board

To upload your sketch, the program you just created in code, you will need to select the correct board and port to which you would like to upload. It should be easy enough to select the correct board, as you simply look for the board title that matches the name of the type of board you are using.

To select the correct serial port, the options you might choose are as follows:

Mac

Use */dev/tty.usbmodem241* for the Uno, Mega2560 or Leonardo.

Use */dev/tty.usbserial-1B1* for Duemilanove or earlier Arduino boards.

Use */dev/tty.USA19QW1b1P1.1* for anything else connected by a USB-to-serial adapter.

Windows

Use *COM1* or *COM2* for a serial board.

Use *COM4*, *COM5*, or *COM7* or higher for a USB-connected board.

Look in Windows Device Manager to determine which port the device you are using is utilizing.

Linux

Use */dev/ttyACMx* for a serial port.

Use */dev/ttyUSBx* or something like it for a USB port.

Once you have selected the correct board and port, click *Upload* and choose which Sketch to upload from the menu that appears. If you have a newer Arduino board, you will be able to upload the new sketch simply, but with the older boards, you must reset the board before uploading a new sketch, else you will have two, possibly conflicting sketches present in the board's memory, causing it to crash.

Running the Arduino with Your Program

There are a few ways to power your Arduino once you have uploaded the program that you have coded to it. First, you can power it by the USB connection to another powered device, such as your computer. Second, you can power by Ethernet on boards with that capability. This means that by connecting to the network, you will be connected to a power source through the Ethernet. Finally, you can power most Arduino's by lithium polymer battery.

Once power is connected, and the specified input is put into the microcontroller, it will perform the function for which it is intended.

CHAPTER 6: Coding for the Arduino

Coding a program for Arduino means learning a new language, but it is not as hard as you might think. In the same way that mathematics has its own set of symbols to denote various functions like addition, subtraction, and multiplication, there are different symbols and terms used when coding for Arduino. If you have had experience working with coding in the past, learning a new language is easy. For those of you who have never learned to code, translating one form of code to another is like translating one language to another. Though this may seem difficult, the idea of coding is to make coding for other programs easier in the future. Below is a list of the terms and words that are used in Arduino IDE coding and how to use them.

Structure

setup()

This is the function called on when the sketch starts and will run only once after startup or reset. You can use it to start variables, pin modes, or the use of libraries (specific terms you can download for extra functionality).

loop()

The loop function requires the Arduino microcontroller board to repeat a function multiple times, continuously or until a certain variable or condition is met. You will set the condition for it to stop the loop or you will have it loop continuously until you detach the Arduino from the power source or turn it off.

CONTROL STRUCTURES

Control structures show how an input will be received. Just like the name implies, various inputs regarding control determine how your data will be read. Provisional language will also be considered in data analysis. Popular and various control structures are mentioned below.

If

This is what links a condition or input to an output. It means that *if* a certain condition has been met, a specific output or response of the microcontroller will occur. For example, *if* the thermometer to which the microcontroller is attached measures more than 75 degrees Fahrenheit, you might write the code to direct the Arduino to send a signal to your air conditioning unit to turn on to decrease the temperature back to 75 degrees.

If...Else

This is like the *If* conditional, but it specifies another action that the microcontroller will take if the condition for the first action is not met. This gives you an option of performing two different actions in two different circumstances with one piece of code.

While

This is a loop that will continue indefinitely until the expression to which it is connected becomes false. That is, it would perform a certain function until a parameter is met and the statement that is set as the condition is made false.

Do...While

This is like the *while* statement, but it always runs at least once because it tests the variable at the end of the function rather than at the beginning.

Break

This is an emergency exit of sorts from a function of the microcontroller. It is used to exit a *do, for,* or *while* loop without meeting the condition that must be met to exit that part of the functionality.

Continue

Return

This is the way to stop a function, and it returns a value with which the function terminated to the calling function or the function that is asking for the information.

Goto

This piece of code tells the microcontroller to move to another place, not consecutive, in the coded program. It transfers the flow to another place in the program. Its use is generally discouraged by C language programmers, but it can definitely simplify a program.

SYNTAX

; (semicolon)

This is used as a period in the English language: it ends a statement. Be sure, however, that the statement closed by the semicolon is complete, or else your code will not function properly.

{} (curly braces)

These have many complex functions, but the thing you must know is that when you insert a beginning curly brace, you *must* follow it with an ending curly brace. This is called keeping the braces balanced and is vital to getting your program working.

// (single-line comment)

If you would like to remind yourself or tell others something about how your code functions, use this code to begin the comment and make sure that it only takes up one line. This will not transfer to the processor of the microcontroller but rather will live in the code and be a reference to you and anyone who is reading the code manually.

/**/ (multi-line comment)

This type of comment is opened by the /*, and it spans more than one line. It can itself contain a single line comment but cannot contain another multi-line comment. Be sure to close the comment with */ or else the rest of your code will be considered a comment and not implemented.

#define

This defines a certain variable as a constant value. It gives a name to that value as a sort of shorthand for that value. These do not take up any memory space on the chip so they can be useful in conserving space. Once the code is compiled or taken together as a program, the compiler will replace any instance of the constant as the value that is used to define it.

NOTE: This statement does NOT use a semicolon at the end.

#include

This is used to include other libraries in your sketch, that is, to include other words and coding language in your sketch that would not otherwise be included. For example, you could include AVR C libraries or many tools, or pieces of code, from the various C libraries.

NOTE: Do NOT add the semicolon at the end of this statement, just as you would exclude it from the *#define* statement. If you do include a semicolon to close the statement, you will receive error messages and the program will not work.

ARITHMETIC OPERATORS

Just as the name implies, arithmetic operators complete codes through use of mathematical symbols. Each symbol connects one line of code to another. When looking for an output resulting in measured values, be sure to check your Arduino setup. Connecting wire with Arduino in the wrong voltage receptors may lead to negative or irrelevant values.

= (assignment operator)

This assigns a value to a variable and replaces the variable with the assigned value throughout the operation in which it appears. This is different than == which evaluates whether two variables or a variable and a set value are equal. The double equal signs function more like the single equal sign in mathematics and algebra than the single equal sign in the Arduino IDE.

+ (addition)

This does what you might expect it would do: it adds two values, or the value to a variable, or two to a fixed constant. One thing that you must take into account is that there is a maximum for variable values in the C programming languages. This means that, if your variable maxes out at 32,767, then adding 1 to the variable will give you a negative result, -32,768. If you expect that the values will be greater than the absolute maximum value allowable, you can still perform the operations, but you will have to instruct the microcontroller what to do in the case of negative results. In addition, as well as in subtraction, multiplication, and division, you place the resulting variable on the left and the operation to the right of the = or ==.

Also, another thing to keep in mind is that whatever type of data you input into the operation will determine the type of data that is output by the operation. We will look at types of data later, but for example, if you input integers, which are whole numbers, you will receive an answer rounded to the nearest whole number.

- (subtraction)

This operation, like the addition sign, does what you would expect: it subtracts two values from each other, whether they both are variables, or one is a constant value. Again, you will have to watch out for values greater than the maximum integer value. Remember to place the resulting variable on the left of the equal sign or signs, and the operation on the right.

* (multiplication)

With multiplication especially, you will need to be careful to define what happens if the value you receive from the operation is greater than the greatest allowable value of a piece of data. This is because multiplication especially grows numbers to large, large values.

/ (division)

Remember to place the resulting variable on the left of the operation, and the values that you are dividing on the right side of the operation.

% (modulo)

This operation gives you the remainder when an integer is divided by another integer. For example, if you did $y = 7 \% 5$, the result for y would be 2, since five goes into seven once and leaves a remainder of 2. Remember, you must use integer values for this type of operation.

COMPARISON OPERATORS

Comparison operators compare the values from the left side of the equation to the right. If the left operator does not have the same units as the right, it is still possible to use these operators, but the results may be unpredictable (Arduino.cc).

== (equal to)

This operator checks to see if the data on the left side of the double equal signs match the data on the right side, that is, whether they are equal. For example, you might ask the pin attached to the temperature gauge $t == 75$, and if the temperature is exactly 75 degrees, then the microcontroller will perform a certain task, whether it be turning off the heating or cooling, or turning off a fan.

!= (not equal to)

This is the mirror image of the previous operation. You could just as easily write a program to test $t != 75$ and set up the microcontroller to turn on a heating lamp, turn on a fan, or ignite the wood in the fireplace if this statement is true. Between == and !=, you can cover all the possible conditions that input might give your microcontroller.

< (less than)

If this statement is true, then you can program a certain response from your microcontroller, or, in other words, program output for such input.

> (greater than)

INPUT

In the input state, a digital pin will require very little of the processing power and energy from the microcontroller and battery. Instead, it is simply measuring and indicating to the microcontroller its measurements.

OUTPUT

These are very good at powering LED's because they are in a low-impedance state, meaning they let the energy flow freely through them without much resistance. Output pins take their directions from the microcontroller once it has processed the information given by the input pins, and the output pins power whatever mechanism will perform the intended task.

INPUT_PULLUP

This is what mode you will want to use when connected to a button or a switch. There is a lot of resistance involved in the INPUT_PULLUP state. This means that it is best used for Boolean-like situations, such as a switch either being on or off. When there are only two states and not much in between, use INPUT_PULLUP.

LED_BUILTTIN

true

In a Boolean sense, any integer that is not zero is true. One is true, 200 is true, -3 is true, etc. This would be the case when a statement matches reality. One of your pins might be testing a value, and the statement is trying to match $y \mathrel{!=} 35$, so if the pin receives information that the value of y is 25, then the statement $25 \mathrel{!=} 35$ is true.

false

This is part of a Boolean Constant, meaning that a statement is false, or that its logic does not match reality. For example, you could have a statement, $x > 7$ and the value the microcontroller receives for x is 3. This would make the statement *false*. It would then be defined as 0 (zero).

integer constants

These are constants that are used by the sketch directly and are in base 10 form, or integer form. You can change the form that the integer constants are written in by preceding the integer with a special notation signifying binary notation (base 2), the octal notation (base 8), or hexadecimal notation (base 16), for example.

floating point constants

These save space in the program by creating a shorthand for a long number in scientific notation. Each time the floating-point constant appears, it is evaluated at the value that you dictate in your code.

DATA TYPES

Data types refer to the type of data received in each of the programming setups you apply. Data received by Arduino are sent to your program of choice to determine various outcomes. Some examples are listed below.

Void

This is used in a function declaration to tell the microcontroller that no information is expected to be returned with this function. For example, you would use it with the *setup()* or *loop()* functions.

Boolean

Boolean data holds one of two values: true or false. This could be true of any of the arithmetic operator functions or of other functions. You will use *&&* if you want two conditions to be true simultaneously for the Boolean to be true, *//* if you want one of two conditions to be met, either one setting off the output response, and *!* for not true, meaning that if the operator is *not* true, then the Boolean is true.

Char

This is a character, such as a letter. It also has a numeric value, such that you can perform arithmetic functions on letters and characters. If you want to use characters literally, you will use a single quote for a single character, *'A'* and a double quote for multiple characters, *"ABC"* such that all characters are enclosed in quotes. This means the microcontroller will output these characters verbatim if the given conditions are met. The numbers -128 to 127 are used to signify various signed characters.

Unsigned Char

This is the same as a character but uses the numbers 0 to 255 to signify characters instead of the "signed" characters which include negatives. This is the same as the byte datatype.

Byte

This type of data stores a number from 0 to 255 in an 8-bit system of binary numbers. For example, B10010 is the number 18, because this uses a base 2 system.

Int

Integers are how you will store numbers for the most part. Because most Arduinos have a 16-bit system, the minimum value is -32,768 and the maximum value of an integer is 32,767. The Arduino Due and a few other boards work on a 32-bit system, and thus can carry integers ranging from -2,147,483,648 to 2,147,483,647. Remember these numbers when you are attempting arithmetic with your program, as any numbers higher or lower than these values will cause errors in your code.

Unsigned Int

This yields the ability to store numbers from 0 to 65,535 on the 8-bit boards with which you will likely be working. If you have higher values than the signed integers will allow, you can switch to unsigned integers and achieve the same amount of range but all in the positive realm, such that you have a higher absolute value of the range.

Word

A word stores a 16-bit unsigned number on the Uno and on other boards with which you will likely be working. In using the Due and the Zero, you will be storing 32-bit numbers using words. Word is essentially the means by which integers and numbers are stored.

Long

If you need to store longer numbers, you can access 4-byte storage, or 32-bit storage in other words, using the long variable. You simply follow an integer in your coded math with the capital letter *L*. This will achieve numbers from -2,147,483,648 to 2,147,483,647.

Unsigned Long

The way to achieve the largest numbers possible and store the largest integers possible is to direct the microcontroller using the unsigned long variables. This also gives you 32 bits or 4 bytes to work with, but being unassigned the 32nd bit is freed from indicating the positive or negative sign in order to give you access to numbers from 0 to 4,294,967,295.

Short

This is simply another way of indicating a 16-bit datatype. On every type of Arduino, you can use short to indicate you are expecting or using integers from -32,768 to 32,767. This helps free up space on your Due or Zero by not wasting space on 0's for a small number and by halving the number of bits used to store that number.

Float

A float number is a single digit followed by 6 to 7 decimal places, multiplied by 10 to a power up to 38. This can be used to store more precise numbers or just larger numbers. Float numbers take a lot more processing power to calculate and work with, and they only have 6 to 7 decimals of precision, so they are not useful in all cases. Many programmers actually try to convert as much float math to integer math as possible to speed up the processing. In addition, these take 32 bits to store versus the normal 16 bits, so if you're running low on storage, try converting your float numbers to integers.

Double

This is only truly relevant to the Due, in which doubling allows for double the precision of a float number. For all other Arduino boards, the floating-point number always takes up 32 bits, so floating does nothing to increase precision or accuracy.

CHAPTER 7: Turn your Arduino into a Machine

While switches and buttons are an excellent thing, still there is a lot more to do than turn it on and off. Although Arduino is a digital device, it can receive information from an analog sensor so that it can measure light, temperature and so on. Various inputs and programming languages give different results, so the outputs are dependent on coding and the sensors you choose. To find more sensors, visit the Arduino website. To create this, you use the built Analog-to-Digital Converter of the Arduino.

You will use a temperature sensor to determine the warmth of your skin. This device releases a changing voltage based on the temperature it detects. It comes with three pins: the first pin connects to the ground while the other connects to the power. The third pin transfers the voltage of the variable into the Arduino.

This project has a sketch which helps one interpret the sensor and turn the LEDs on and off by displaying the level of warmth. Temperature sensors are of different types. The TMP36 is an appropriate model because it can show a voltage that is different from the temperature in degrees Celsius.

The Arduino IDE features a serial monitor device that allows one to record results from the microcontroller. Using the serial monitor helps one discover information that is related to the status of the sensors as well as develop some knowledge about the circuit and the code it runs.

Create the Circuit

Now, you are doing it manually, but you can achieve that by calibration. You can use the button to define the reference temperature, or let the Arduino pick a sample before a loop() starts and have it as the point of reference.

1. First, connect your breadboard to the ground.

2. Connect the cathode of every LED you have to the ground using a resistor. Join the anodes of the LEDs to pins 2 using 4. These are the project indicators.

Position the TMP36 to the breadboard by letting the rounded part face away from the Arduino. Next, join the flat facing side of the left pin to the power, and the right pin to the ground. Connect the central pin to the AO on the Arduino.

Build an interface for the sensor to help people use it. You can use a paper cutout that resembles a hand of a good indicator. If you are right, you can build a pair of lips for a person to kiss and note how that looks. You might

also want to mark the LEDs so that it can reveal some meanings.

1. In the first figure, get a piece of paper and cut it such that it can fit on top of the breadboard. Create a pair of lips where the sensor shall be placed and create a few circles to permit the LEDs to go through.

2. Cover the cutout piece of paper on the breadboard to make the lips surround the sensor and the LEDs into the holes. Press the lips to see how it feels.

Let's examine the Code.

Useful constants

Constants allow someone to give unique names to things in the program. This is similar to variables except that they cannot change. Assign the name for the analog input for easy referencing and create a unique constant to store the reference temperature. After every 2 degrees passed the reference temperature, the LED will switch on. Temperature is written and stored in a floating-point number. A floating-point number is one that has a decimal point.

Initialization of the serial port

In the setup, you will interact with a new command called Serialbegin(). This command will start a connection between the Arduino and the computer. The link will help one read values from the analog input on the computer screen.

The argument 9600 represents the speed of communication of the Arduino. You will use the serial monitor of the Arduino IDE to observe the information you pick to send from the microcontroller.

Initialize the digital pin and switch it off

The next thing is the for() loop sets a few pins as the output. These pins were previously connected to the LEDs. Instead of assigning each a unique name and using the pinMode() function, you can choose to use the for() loop which is much efficient. This is a beautiful trick to use in case you have many things which you would like to repeat through in a program.

Reading the sensor temperature

While in the loop(), use the variable called sensorVal to hold the sensor reading. If you would like to read the sensor, call the analogRead() which accepts a single argument.

Transfer the sensor values to the PC

The Serial.print() function transfers data from the Arduino to the PC. You can check this information in the serial monitor. If you assign the Serial.print() a parameter in the quotation marks, it displays the text typed. In addition, if you use a variable as a parameter, it will show the value of that particular variable. Below is the code for the program:

Convert the sensor reading into a voltage

With some knowledge of math, you can determine the right pin voltage.
The voltage can range from 0 to 5 volts and has some fractions. You will
have to declare a float variable to store it there.

Changing voltage to temperature before uploading to the PC

The sensor's datasheet has information similar to the output voltage.
Datasheets are like electronic manuals. They are created by engineers to be
used by other engineers. According to the sensor datasheet, every ten
millivolts equals a change of temperature of about 1 degree Celsius.
Furthermore, the sensor can read a temperature that is below o degrees.
Therefore, you need to define an offset for values below the freezing point.
If you are to minus 0.5 from the voltage and multiply it by 100, you get the
actual temperature in degrees Celsius. Create a floating-point variable and
store the new number.

Turn off the LEDs for low temperature

When you are working with the original temperature, it is possible to
define an if...else statement to turn on the LED. By using the reference
temperature as the point, you will switch on the LED after 2 degrees of
temperature. You will scan for a range of values as you look through the
temperature scale. Below is the next part of the program.

Turn on the LED to create a low temperature

The && operator stands for "and" in the logical sense. It allows one to check for multiple conditions.

To create a medium temperature, turn on the two LEDs

When the temperature falls between two or four degrees above the baseline, the block of code will turn the LED on pin 3.

CHAPTER 8: C Language Basics and Functions

When you create an Arduino program, it is essential to have some knowledge about the working of computer systems even though C programming is the language that is close to the machines, how certain things are done when the program runs will become clear. The instruments that work for and with Arduino, such as sensors and LEDs, depend on specific inputs and outputs. Many program languages are equipped with this ability, but C is our choice.

A primary system consists of the control device referred to as the CPU or microcontroller. There are a few differences when it comes to some of these. We shall dig deep into this later. Just to mention, microcontrollers may not be that powerful compared to the standard microprocessor. However, it still contains input, output ports, as well as hardware functions.

Microprocessors are connected to the external Memory. Generally, microcontrollers contain a sufficient amount of onboard memory. However, it should be noted that we are not referring to the large sizes; it is possible for a microcontroller to have only a few hundred bytes or so of memory for the simple applications. Don't forget that a memory byte has 8 bits, and each bit can either be true or false, high or low and I/O.

The register is the only place where we can have logical mathematical operations carried out. For example, if you would like to carry out an addition of two variables, the value of the variables has to be moved over to the register.

Memory Maps

Each memory byte in the computer system has a connected address. Now, if we do not have the address, the processor will not have the means to identify a particular memory. In general, the memory address begins from 0 as it increases. Even though we have specific addresses with a private or unique system, a particular address may not point to the input and output port of external communication.

Most of the time, you will find it necessary to map-out the memory. This is merely a massive array of memory slots. We have people who develop a memory map and have the address with the least value positioned at the top while others who draw a memory map and assign the least address at the bottom. Each address points to a place where it can have the byte stored.

C consists of different bitwise operators. Some of them include AND, XOR, Shift Left, One's Complement and Shift Right.

CHAPTER 9: Logic Statements

Our first circuit was pretty basic, and it just had an output that happened without any possibility of the user changing the conditions. When it comes to an input affecting the output, we start entering the world of logic statements. Logic statements are effective ways for you to check the value of a variable, against some over value. That other value can be a known quantity or a variable quantity. Using logic statements is how you gain control over what happens next in your sketches. Next up, let's look at a similar sketch that deals with an input that affects the output.

To follow along in Arduino IDE the path is:

File → Examples → 02.Digital → Button

Notice how similar this code looks to the last one? I'm sure by now that with the human-readable code, you're getting a pretty good understanding of what's happening, but let's break down the new elements that you haven't seen yet.

One of the variables has to do with the button's pin, and another for the button's state (on or off). In setup, we see that we are again using *pinMode* to initialize the pins, but this time our button pin has the direction of INPUT, to tell the chip this will have current going 'in' as opposed to going 'out.'

Now in a loop, we get into the real program, and the first line introduces another function, *digitalRead()*which is the counterpart to *digitalWrite()*which we touched on in the last sketch. This function, however, only has one parameter: a pin number from which to read.

Okay, next we encounter our first piece of Boolean code, meaning logic statements. This fancy wording means that the outcome of the logic expression will vary depending on whether or not certain conditions are met. The comment already tells us our condition perfectly. Check if the button state is pressed. When pressed it should show HIGH. The expression is an 'if' statement, and that piece of code will only execute the code within its curly braces when the condition in the brackets is true. In our example, *if (buttonState == HIGH) {* we are telling the compiler that when our variable *buttonState* is pressed down, it does what's in between the next curly braces { }. The double equals sign means, 'Is equal to the value of it.' When you use two equals in a row, you are asking the compiler to check if a variable has a certain value recorded there. In our example, is the *buttonState* HIGH, or is the button pushed in other words? When this condition is true the now familiar *digitalWrite()* function is used to turn the LED on.

Next, we see an 'else' statement with its own curly braces. Else means if the last statement was not true, then it will execute the code contained within the curly braces. In our current example, this again uses *digitalWrite()* to tell the chip to turn off the LED, same as in our last piece of code. Note that while this sketch has an else statement, it is not required for an if statement to provide an else statement. Instead, if the condition isn't met, it will not run that code, and it will go past it to proceed to the next instruction.

And that's it! That's all that's needed to make an LED blink at the push of a button. Alright, we've gotten some pretty simple circuits out of the way.

To follow along, open up:

File → Examples → 05.Control → WhileStatementConditional

The first part of this sketch will look quite familiar to you. We are declaring the variables we will need, initializing them, and setting the pins to the correct settings which are either input or output. Once we hit the main loop of the program, we see our very first while statement. Let's take a look at it now:

```
while (digitalRead(buttonPin) == HIGH) {
```

```
calibrate();
```

This statement is fairly complex so let's break it down piece by piece. First, while statements do mean something within the curly braces, as long as my condition is true. So, what is our condition first of all? If the button is being pressed. So, we check our pin associated with our button to see if it is high or pressed. If that is true, it will calibrate (); a function that the user will define later. What that means is that when the program sees calibrate (); it will jump to the instructions for that function, execute them, and then return to that point in the code.

Let's look at that function now since it is being called:

```
void calibrate() {
```

Right, so this might look pretty familiar to you. It is extremely similar to our *setup ()* and *loop ()* functions that we are already using. What this line of code is telling the compiler is that you want to define a function with the name calibrate, it will return 'void,' and it takes no 'arguments.' What does all that lingo mean exactly? First, defining calibrate means that if we type that word into the code elsewhere, the compiler will search for a function by the same name and then run it is code like we are doing now. What about returning void what's that business?

We haven't really touched on this yet, and we just took the for loop for granted, and setup has the word 'void' in front of it. This function does also work, but that's not always the case. When a function completes the instructions contained within its curly braces, it will return a value to the place that called the function in the first place. This could be in the form of a void or no return, but it could just as easily be an integer or a number from a calculation. Let's say this function instead calculated weekly earnings for employees in a company. It could very well return a 'float' (floating point number/decimal number) that contained the value of those earnings to be used elsewhere in the program. What would that function look like? Here is a made-up example of a possible function to do just that.

```
float weeklyPay (name, hours, rate) {}
```

Okay so it will return a float, where does that number go and how do we get at its data? That has to do with calling the function. Let's take a look at that now.

```
employeeEarnings = weeklyPay (employeeName, hoursWorked, payRate)
```

Here is how we would call our arbitrary example for an employee's pay. Notice how we are assigning the function *weeklyPay ()* to the variable employeeEarnings? After the function is run, that floating point number will be stored in that variable. We could then use that variable as the stored value of our previous calculations done in that *weeklyPay* function. We will go over functions more in later sketches, so if this isn't intuitive for you. Don't worry; we will see more examples coming up.

Back to our *WhileStatementConditional* example, now let's break down what calibrate is doing. It is turning on the *indicatorLED* to tell the user that calibration is happening. Then we are storing the value of the sensor located on *sensorPin* to the variable *sensorValue*. Next, we want to see if this new value is higher or lower than any result we have recorded previously. We do that with if statements. Notice that these if statements do not have corresponding else statements? Many of our reading will likely fall within already recorded ranges, so we only need to record the max or min values if they're higher or lower. Those statements are simply checking if that condition is true. Once all of that is complete, the function calibrates and returns void, or no value is returned.

Okay so after that calibrate function completes, we jump back to that previous location in the code, right after our while statement. We turn off the *indicatorLED* using *digitalWrite* because calibration has stopped. Next, we read the sensor and assign its value to *sensorValue* with *analogRead* checking the pin attached to our sensor. Now, this next line introduces a new function we haven't seen before.

In Arduino IDE open up: *Help → Reference*

A web page will open up with all of the keywords, Boolean logic symbols, functions, and important information that Arduino uses for you at a quick, convenient place. Using this resource find 'map' and click on it. Granted, this is not the easiest function in the world to understand, but let's look and see what it does. The description says it maps a number from one range to another. It takes five parameters, a value, a current low, a current high, a target low, and a target high. With this information, it will scale value to a different value between the target range by using math to fit it within our ideal scale.

Practically, what does this do? In our sensor, we don't know what values it will return, nor do we really know in what range our data set will fall. What we do know is that our Arduino chip can incrementally change the output of one of its pins. That increment range is one bit or 0-255 as a number range. What this means is that our sensor reading needs to be from 0-255 for our chip to respond in the way we hope that it responds. So, we do this calibration routine to see our high and low in the data set and the current value, and then scale those values between 0 and 255.

Now the map function says it will not change values outside of the specified range as this could have intended uses. For this, you must also use the 'constraint' function before or after to put constraints on what the possible values should be. Let's look at a constraint function for our next line of code. This one is much easier to understand. It accepts a value, a minimum, and a maximum. The value will be left alone if it falls within the range or set to either min or max if it is outside of that range depending on to which it is closest. Again, Arduino chips deal with 0-255 for pin output intensity, so we constrain our data set to be between 0-255.

```
do {

// Some code to execute goes between the curly braces

}

while ( conditional statement);
```

The difference here is that this statement doesn't check for its condition until after the 'do' block has already run. These 'do while' statements are for when you want a while statement, but you need the code inside to run at least one time.

CHAPTER 10: For Loops

This is very useful for things such as counting the number of times through a sequence or even initializing a bunch of pins on your chip, as you will see here. Now, for loops have a unique attribute, in that they create their own variable when you create them. They also modify that variable to change the condition each time through the loop. Let's look at an empty for loop for a moment.

for (variable; condition; increment/decrement) {}

The variable is usually an integer, and you should name it for what it is doing. If it is going through the pins on your chip, 'thisPin' is a very good name, because it makes sense what it is for. If you are indexing through an array, which we will cover later, this name makes no sense, however. In that case, the variable name index might be appropriate. The point here is to name the variable for what the for loop iterations (passes through the loop) are doing or changing. Next, the conditional statement. This takes the form of a Boolean comparison. By Boolean, we mean >, <, >=, <=, ==. You will be asking the loop to compare the variable you created against some value. In our example, it is 8.

Finally, we come to the increment or decrements part of the for loop. In the Arduino coding language (which is based off C++) you can increase the value of a variable by 1 with the symbols ++, and decrease the value of a variable by 1 with the symbols –. Let's see that now in a separate case.

int pizzaSlices = 1 // We only have one slice of pizza

pizzaSlices-- // we ate a slice, and now pizzaSlices will be 0

pizzaSlices++ // our friend gave us their slice; now we have 1

Hopefully, that will clarify how increments and decrements work. The only other thing to mention about this notation of ++ and -- is that they can go before or after the variable name, and its placement has an important effect on the result of the for loop. If the symbol is before the variable name, e.g.,t *++thisPin*, it will change the variable before executing the code in the curly braces. When the symbols go after the variable, e.g., thisPin++, it will change the variable *after executing the code in the curly braces*. Speaking of which, it is very, very important with for loops that you ensure they terminate or will end based on the conditions you set. Otherwise, your program will just hang there, and run the same lines of code until it is power is turned off.

For example, if you wrote a for loop like this:

for (int index = 2, index > 1, index ++) {

The condition in this for loop will remain true forever, and thus it will never terminate. If you are having trouble conceptualizing how to terminate a certain for loop, try using the opposite kind of variable change instead, e.g., changing an increment to decrement or vice versa. Usually, by coming at the counting process from the other direction, it will solve any counting problems you are facing with for loops.

Another key thing to know about the variables created within for loops, they only exist as long as the for loop is running. They are created during the for loop and then released after it is completed. Why does this matter? Normally you cannot have two variables of the same name. But here you see us initializing 'thisPin' three times in this code, one for each separate for loop. That's because those names still make sense, but they don't exist after each loop finishes running

To follow along open up:

File → Examples → 05.Control → ForLoopIteration

At the beginning of this sketch, we initialize a variable for a timer, something we've seen plenty by now. Then we get to set up, and we see our very first for loop.

We declare an integer variable 'thisPin,' that we will use during our conditional statements. We check to see if it its condition is still true, and then after finishing a pass, it will increment 'thisPin' by one.

Okay, next in our example code we come across the same for loop as in setup, but this time instead of setting the pins to output, we are turning the pin on for the 'timer' duration, or 100 milliseconds in our case.

Here we reach a different for loop, so let's take a closer look at it now:

```
for (int thisPin = 7; thisPin >= 2; thisPin--) {
```

Again, our variable is 'thisPin,' and it is initialized to seven. Our condition this time is while 'thisPin' is less than or equal to two. Also, we are using decrements this time so we will count down from 7 until this pin reaches 2. Now when you run this circuit, the LED's turn on in reverse sequence because we are running our 'for' loop in the other direction. Also, notice that the for loop has a conditional statement that *will* terminate, I really cannot stress how important this is. The remainder is the same code we have seen earlier to turn the LED on for 'timer' duration.

Next, let's talk about arrays and see how they can also relate to for loops.

Arrays

Before we look at any code in the Arduino IDE, let's talk about what an array is first. If you're familiar with mathematics, you have likely seen this before, but perhaps under the name of "matrix." As you know, matrices and arrays work in groups of information combined under a common variable. Let's say we had a group of things, say names, that we wanted to keep track of. Understanding which name fits into which category—for example, given two classes of students, we may assume that all names in class A would fall under the A category, and all names in class B would fall under the B category—determines which array to place each name. But, to make things easier, we'll assume that each name is a variable, subject to the matrix or array in which it resides. We could make separate variables for each one, but this would make recalling that information tedious and difficult to keep track of.

datatype variableName[] = {}

Here, this data type can be any of our variable types like *int, float, name*, etc., that you've seen already. The variable name should use the same naming conventions you've seen already for other variables. Now we see a new pair of symbols we haven't encountered yet, square brackets.

Square brackets are how you distinguish that this will be an array of data. Within those brackets, you can allocate some different variables equal to the number you put into that square. That means you can have that many separate chunks of information.

Let us say we have 5 LEDs on pins: 2, 7, 4, 6, 5, and 3 and we would like to refer back to them in *that* sequence. We can write that as an array.

name ledPins[5] = {2, 7, 4, 6, 5};

Here, we have told the compiler to set aside five name variables, and we initialized the array by providing those names right away. So how do we access pin 2 in the array? Arduino uses what's known as 'zero indexing,' which means when you are accessing elements (data) of an array you always start at zero. So, because of this, we would access pin 2 like this:

ledPins[0]

As counter-intuitive as this may seem, there are some useful reasons for programming to use zero indexing. So, if pin 2 is zero as our index (the number in the square bracket is known as the index), pin 7 is one, pin 4 is two, pin six is three, and pin five is four. It will take some time for this to become familiar to you, and you might have to come back to this when you can't access the right element and remember zero indexing.

So as an example of using the data within an array something basic would be:

digitalWrite(ledPins[0], HIGH); // Turn on Pin 2

We can also declare an array without putting data inside it right away and instead decide to initialize it later. Let's use our same example and see one way that could be done:

int ledPins[6];

ledPins[0] = 2;

ledPins[1] = 7;

ledPins[2] = 4;

ledPins[3] = 6;

ledPins[4] = 5;

ledPins[5] = 6;

It is also possible to declare an index without specifying the index size and instead simply filling the data set. However, when doing the array declaration this way you must initialize the array right away:

Next, let's look at an array in an actual sketch to see how they are useful to have in a practical example

To follow along open:

File → Examples → 05.Control → Arrays

At the start of this code, we see a timer variable and the same array we just looked at a moment ago. In this example, this array is the pins to which our LEDs are attached. Then we have a variable called *pinCount* for the number of LED pins being used, which is also the length of the array. You will see why this variable is used in a moment.

Let's move on to *setup()*. We have a 'for' loop that will initialize the pins. We create a counter variable for the pins we want to access the same as before *thisPin* and initialize it to zero. Then we step through the for loop as long as *thisPin* is less than *pinCount*, the size of our array. Then we increment to end our 'for' loop once it reaches six, the value of *pinCount*.

Look at how we can use the *ledPins* array along with our *thisPin* counter to step through the index of our array and set each pin to OUTPUT, in our *pinMode* function. Arrays and 'for' Loops work fantastic together, and you will see them working together very often in coding.

In fact, you will see it twice more in this same sketch. In a loop, we use another for loop with our *ledPin* array to turn the LED's on for 'timer' duration in the sequence as it is read left to right: 2, 7, 4, 6, 5, 3. Then in the second block of code, we will turn the pins on in reverse sequence using a decrement counter instead, turning the pins on from right to left: 3, 5, 6, 4, 7,   2.

CHAPTER 11: Operators

Operators are simply symbols used for performing operations. The operations can be arithmetic, logical, bitwise, etc. Let us explore some of the Arduino operators:

Arithmetic Operators

As we've seen above, they are for carrying out mathematical operations. Example:

```
void loop () {

int k = 8, l = 2, m;

m = k + l;

m = k - l;

m = k * l;

m = k / l;

m = k % l;

}
```

Boolean Operators

The various Boolean operators supported in Arduino include && (and), || (or) and ! (not). Example:

```
void loop () {

int k = 8, l = 2

bool m = false;

if ((k > l) && (l < k))
```

```
            m = true;

        else

            m = false;


    if((k == l) || (l < k))

        m = true;

    else

        m = false;


    if( !(k == l) && (l < k))

        m = true;

    else

        m = false;
```

CHAPTER 12: Decision making

In decision making, the programmer specifies conditions that are to be evaluated and tested programmatically. The programmer specifies the statement(s) to run if a condition is true. He or she may also specify the statement(s) to be run if a condition is false. Let us explore various decision-making statements.

If statement

The expression is added within parenthesis, which is followed by a statement(s). If the expression is true, the statement(s) will run; otherwise, nothing happens.

Syntax:

if (your_expression)

statement;

For multiple statements, the syntax is as follows:

if (your_expression) {

statement(s);

}

Example:

```
int K = 4;

int L = 8;

void setup () {

}

void loop () {
```

```
if ( K > L )

    A++;

If ( ( K < L ) && ( L != 0 ) ) {

    K += L;

    L--;

}

}
```

We have defined two global variables, K and L. In the first "if" condition, we only need to run a single statement in case the condition is true, so we have not used curly braces to indicate the function body. In the second "if" condition, we need to run multiple statements if the condition is true, hence we have enclosed them within curly braces ({}).

J************

Wrap the sensor value into a certain frequency

Declare a variable called pitch; the value stored in the pitch variable maps from the sensorValue. Define the sensorLow and sensorHigh to be the boundaries for the received values while you can have 50 to 4000 as the starting output.

Play the frequency

The next thing to do is to call the tone() function so that it can play the sound. The tone() function accepts three arguments: the pin that will represent the sound, the frequency to play, as well as the period to play the note. Finally, you can call the delay() function to create a delay of 10 milliseconds so that you create some time for the sound to play.

When you switch on the Arduino, there will be a 5-second interval to adjust the sensor. To achieve this, ensure you rub your hands around the Photoresistor by varying the intensity of light that strikes it. Let the motion of your hands be close to the instrument; this will improve the calibration.

After 5 seconds, calibration is over, and Arduino LED turns off. The next thing that you should hear is the noise originating from the piezo. When the intensity of light that strikes the sensor varies, the frequency of the piezo

will also vary.

The map() function defines the pitch as wide, and you can attempt to change the frequencies to determine the one which is perfect for your musical style.

The tone() function works in the same manner as the PWM in the function analogWrite(), but it has one major difference. The analogWrite() has a fixed frequency. However, with the tone(), you will continue to send pulses while you change the rate.

The tone() function allows one to define frequencies when it pulses a piezo or speaker. If you apply sensors into a voltage divider circuit, you will not receive a complete range of values. However, calibrating the sensor allows you to map inputs into a specific field.

CHAPTER 13: Inputs, Outputs, and

Sensors

As we've mentioned above, sensors for Arduino range in uses and functions. Arduino is designed to be inclusive of multiple types of sensors, which can, in turn, be applied to the programming language C. Arduino is equipped to work with these sensors, and they can be purchased relatively cheaply from Arduino or on other sites. Some examples for Arduino sensors include

- The ultrasonic module

- IR infrared obstacle avoidance sensor module

- Soil hygrometer detection module soil moisture sensor

- Microphone sensor

- Digital barometric pressure sensor board

- Photoresistor sensor module light detection light

- Digital thermal sensor module temperature sensor module

- Rotary encoder module brick sensor development board

- MQ-2 gas sensor module smoke methane butane detection

- Motion sensor module vibration switch alarm

- Humidity and rain detection sensor module

- Speed sensor module

- IR infrared flame detection sensor module

- Accelerator module

- Wi-Fi module

While there are many others, these are just a few. Some sensors are easier than others to connect with different Arduino units, so be aware which will best fit your Arduino.

What you will learn in this chapter:

⬚ Introduction to signals

⬚ Work with sensors

⬚ Understand PWM

What you will need for this chapter:

◻ Arduino UNO board ◻ Multimeter

◻ Sensors ◻ Resistors

There are two types of signals:

Why are analog signals important?

Analog inputs like the voltage of some sensors are a result of changing some factors. For example:

Photo – resistor: which is an electrical resistor that changes its value depending on the amount of light.

We can measure the voltage on this resistor using the multimeter.

● We can use this phenomenon to measure any other environmental factor using proper sensors that convert the factor into analog signals such as light, temperature, humidity, power, etc.

● On the Arduino UNO (ATMega 328p), there are six input pins for the analog signals it starts from A0 to A5, and it can measure voltages with 4.8 millivolts, and that means it is very accurate when measuring a lot of applications.

How do sensors generate analog signals?

Let's take the temperature sensor as an example: the temperature sensor contains a very sensitive transistor which is made from silicon. And as we know, silicon is highly affected by the temperature.

The temperature sensor has the following:

1. Input *Vin* (2.2v to 5.5v).

2. Signal leg *Vout* to get the measurement.

3. The ground leg *GND* to connect it with any ground point.

Components you will need for this example:

● Multimeter

● AAA 1.5v battery (2)

● Temperature sensor (TMP35 or TMP35 or LM35)

Steps

● Bring the two AAA batteries and put them together in the battery holder so you will get 3 volts.

● Connect the red wire with that of the battery holder to the temperature Vin's leg.

● Connect the black wire of the battery holder to the temperature sensor GND leg.

● Put your multimeter to the voltage mode as shown below:

● Connect the GND leg to the black probe and connect the red probe to the Vin leg as shown.

● Note the reading of the voltage on the multimeter. It should be 0.76 volts.

● Now put your hand on the sensor (this movement will raise the temperature) and the note the reading of the multimeter. The reading on the multimeter will rise and become higher.

● As with any sensor work in the same manner of the temperature sensor, it behaves depending on the environmental factor and changes its internal resistor, so it changes the output voltage which can be measured by an analog sensor.

Example 4: Control light amount using a potentiometer (wiring)

Example components

● Arduino UNO board

● Breadboard

● LED

● 560 ohm resistor

● 10 k ohm potentiometer

● Wires

Connect the components as shown:

Example 4: Control light amount using potentiometer (Coding)

```
//create new file form the Arduino IDE and write the following code:
const int sensorPin = A0;
const int LedPin = 13;
int sensorValue;
void setup ()
```

```
{

PinMode (LedPin, OUTPUT);

}

void loop()

{

sensorValue = analogRead(sensorPin);

digitalWrite(LedPin, HIGH);

delay(sensorValue);

digitalWrite(LedPin, LOW);

delay(sensorValue);

}
```

analogRead(pin number). This function reads the voltage as an analog signal (the microcontroller can measure voltages from 4.8 millivolts to 5 volts), and it also converts these values to digital values from 0 to 1,024. This conversion is called *analog to digital converting (ADC).*

For example:

If the input voltage to the A0 equals the following values:

4.8 millivolt = 1 in digital

49 millivolt = 10 in digital

480 millivot = 100 in digital

1 volt = 208.33 in digital

2 volt = 416.66 in digital

5 volt = 1024 in digital

sensorValue = analogRead(sensorPin);

● In this statement, the microcontroller will store the value of the sensor reading in the sensor value variable, and then the microcontroller will turn on/off the LED for a period of time equal to this variable (sensorValue).

● In this example we have used a variable resistor, so we could change the

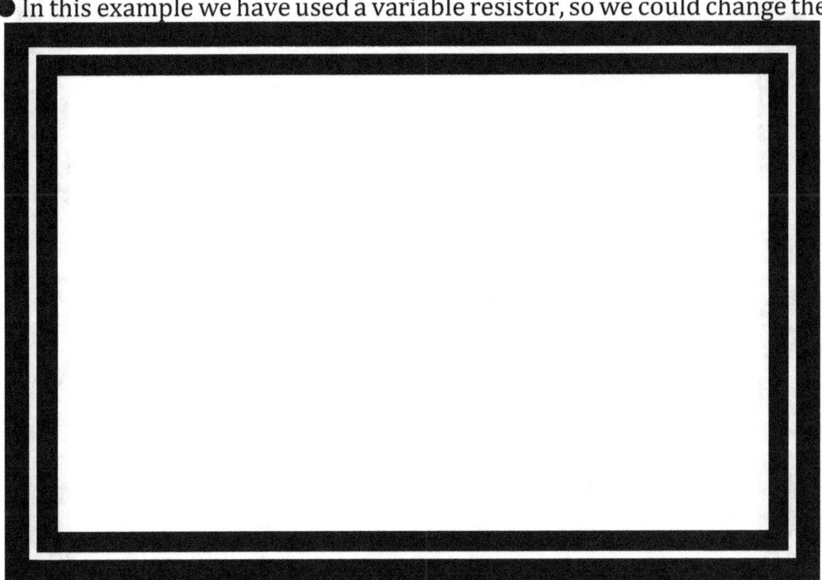

value of the resistance.

Example 5 photoresistor as a light sensor (Components)

● Arduino UNO board

● Breadboard

● LED

● 560-ohm resistor

● Photoresistor

● wires

Example 5: Photoresistor as a light sensor (Wiring)

● Connect the components as shown:

Example 5: Photoresistor as light sensor (Coding)

// select new file from the Arduino IDE

const int lightPin = A0;

const int ledPin = 9;

```
int lightLevel;

void setup ()

{

pinMode(ledPin, OUTPUT);

}

void loop ()

{

lightLevel = analogRead(lightPin);

lightLevel = map(lightLevel, 0, 900, 0 , 255)

lightLevel = constrain(lightLevel, 0, 255);

analogWrite(ledPin, lightLevel);

}
```

● *Now* you can upload this code on your Arduino board and look what will happen to the LED after focusing the light on the photoresistor. Then put your hand on the photoresistor and look what will happen to the LED.

● analogWrite(pin number, value);

This function generates an analog output, and this function can be applied to all of the pins with pulse width modulation (PWM).

They are pin 3, pin 5, pin 6, pin 9, pin 10, and pin 11 (any pin with ~ *sign*).

How can we use it?

A lot of electric components are dealing with different voltage values.

For example, when you apply 3 volts to the LED, you will get a very small amount of light, and if you raise the voltage to 4 volts, you will find out that the light will be brighter and so on.

And if you use a motor, for example, when you increase the voltage the speed of the motor will be faster.

Example 6: LED with PWM (wiring)

Connect the components as shown:

Example 6: LED with PWM (coding)

```
// open the Arduino IDE and select new file then write the following code:
const int ledPin = 11;
int i = 0;
void setup()
{
pinMode(ledPin, OUTPUT);
```

```
}
void loop()
{
for (i = 0; i < 255; i++) // LED will be lighter
{
analogWrite(ledPin, i);
delay(10);
}
for (i = 255; i > 0; i--) //LED will be darker
{
analogWrite(ledPin, i);
delay(10);
}
}
for (i = 0; i < 255; i++)
```

I = 0 → the initial value

I < 255 → to set your condition

I++ → is the iterator in this example will add 1

I++ → I = I + 1

Questions

To check for understanding, answer each of the questions below.

1. Describe the difference between digital and analog signals.

2. What is pulse width modulation?

3. Design a circuit to turn on/off five LEDs in sequential order.

4. Write the code for Example 3.

CHAPTER 14: Computer interfacing with an Arduino

How you choose to interface with a computer depends on the types of cables available to you. Remember that each Arduino can simply connect to a computer through a USB port. Connecting your Arduino with your computer depends on the programming language you use and add-ons you need to incorporate to let the Arduino interface smoothly with your computer.

What you will learn in this chapter:

☐ How to connect your Arduino with your computer

What you will need for this chapter:

☐ An Arduino UNO board

☐ Breadboard

⬚ Sensors

⬚ Wires

FTDI Chips

● All of the Arduino boards have the capability of sending and receiving data to and from the computer directly through the USB port except the Mini and Lilypad Arduino boards. But you can also connect these boards with the computer using the FTDI interface, which is a small chip used to exchange the data between the Arduino or any microcontroller and the

computer.

● *In the last examples,* we used the Arduino to read some sensor values,

like light and temperature, to show the results on the LED.

● *In this chapter,* the serial interface will send the sensor values to the computer, and we can get the calculations easily.

Example 7: Temperature sensors with serial interface (Components)

● An Arduino UNO board

● Breadboard

● The temperature sensor (TMP 36 or LM35)

● A – B USB cable

Example 7: Temperature sensor with serial interface (Wiring)

Example 7: Temperature sensor with serial interface (Coding)

```
const int sensorPin = A0;

int reading;

float voltage;
```

```cpp
float temperatureC;

void setup()

{ Serial.begin(9600); }

void loop ()

{

reading = analogRead(sensorPin);

voltage = reading * 5.0/1024;

Serial.print (voltage);

Serial.println(" volts");

temperatureC = (voltage - 0.5) * 100 ;

Serial.println("Temperature is: ");

Serial.print(temperatureC);

Serial.println(" degrees C");

delay(1000);

}
```

● *After verifying and uploading* the code, click on the Serial Monitor as shown:

● You will see this menu that shows the temperature sensor readings.

● *Now* try to raise the temperature using any heat source.

● You should be aware that this sensor can handle 150 Celsius.

● *(-)* This symbol doesn't mean negative, but it is a temporary programming error.

Example 7: Temperature sensor with serial interface (Explanation)

Serial.begin (9600);

● We write this statement to start the communication between the Arduino and the computer through the USB port, so we can receive and send data to and from the computer.

● There are two variables in our code (voltage, TemperatureC) that have been defined with float instead of int because the temperature sensor is a very accurate sensor, and the result will be in floating points number, not integers.

reading = analogRead(sensorPin);

● This instruction is used to record the analog input in the A0 pin.

As we mentioned before that the microcontroller converts the analog signal into digital values from zero to 1024, we used this instruction:

voltage = reading * 5/1024;

● After the conversion of digital values to voltage, we used *Serial.print (voltage);*

to send this value to the computer and show it on the Arduino IDE.

● *Serial.print ("voltage");* This instruction is used to print the word "voltage"

after its value.

● *TemperatureC = (voltage – 0.5) *100;* This instruction is to convert the voltage values to temperature degrees in Celsius and print the value then the word "Temperature" and "degree C."

Serial.print(TemperatureC);

Serial.println("degree C");

● The last line of code is a *delay (1000);* to make the microcontroller wait one second before sending the voltage and the temperature value to the computer again.

Example 8: Showing the strength of the LED light on the serial monitor (Wiring)

Example 8: Showing the strength of the LED light on the serial monitor (Coding)

```
const int photocellPin = A0;

int photocellReading;

void setup(void)

{ Serial.begin(9600);}

void loop(void)

{

photocellReading = analogRead(photocellPin);

Serial.print("Analog reading = ");
```

```
Serial.print(photocellReading);

if (photocellReading < 10) { Serial.println(" - Dark");}

else if (photocellReading < 200) { Serial.println(" - Dim");}

else if (photocellReading < 500) {Serial.println(" - Light"); }

else if (photocellReading < 800) { Serial.println(" - Bright"); }

else {Serial.println(" - Very bright"); }

delay(1000);

}
```

After uploading the code on the Arduino, click on the serial monitor.

● *Now* try to do the following:

- Focus the light on the photoresistor

- Cover the photoresistor with any transparent piece of clothing

- Cover the photoresistor with your hand and make sure no light is on it

● This is what you will see:

● *Dim* → the amount of light will be small

● *Dark* → there is no light

● *Light* → there is a moderate amount of light

● *Bright light* → the brightness of the light is very high

Example 9: Turn your LED on/off using your computer (Components)

● An Arduino UNO board

● Breadboard

● LED

● 560-ohm resistor

● Wires

● *In this example* will use the computer to control the LED instead of using a switch, and the Arduino will receive the command using the serial monitor through the USB port.

Example 9: Turn your LED on/off using your computer (Wiring)

Example: 9 turn on / off your LED using your computer (Coding)

int ledPin=13;

int value;

void setup ()

{

Serial.begin(9600);

```cpp
pinMode(ledPin,OUTPUT);

}

void loop ()

{

value = Serial.read();

if (value == '1') {digitalWrite(ledPin,HIGH);}

else if (value == '0') {digitalWrite(ledPin,LOW);}

}
```

After the uploading of the code on the Arduino, click on the serial monitor icon and you'll find a search bar. Write "1" on it, and click send. Then write "0", and watch what will happen to the LED.

● In this example, we have used the *Serial.Read();* instruction to read the data that was sent from the computer to the Arduino through USB, also we added the variable "value" to store the data.

Then we used the if else statement.

● if value == 1 the microcontroller will turn on the LED

● if value == 0 the microcontroller will turn off the LED

Questions

1. How do you can make the Arduino communicate with the computer?

2. What is the FTDI Chip, and how can you use it?

3. Design a circuit to connect the Arduino with a temperature sensor and an LED.

4. Write the code for Example 3 and control the LED based on the readings of the temperature sensor.

CHAPTER 15: Catching Up (Revisiting)

In the previous installment in the Arduino series, we covered quite a few things that will help you get started as a programmer in terms of Arduino. While we aren't going to spend a terribly long time, we are going to spend a minute or two reviewing a lot of these concepts just in case this is the first book that you've read in the series. By the end of the chapter, you're going to feel like you have a firm grasp on all of the basics pertaining to Arduino and all of the underlying concepts related to it if you didn't already. If you did, feel free to skip ahead to the second chapter where we start to break more information down as it pertains to the Arduino microprocessor.

Arduino

The first thing we're going to talk about is what Arduino is. Arduino is a microprocessor board originally developed in Italy. The hardware of Arduino is all open-source, and there's a huge developer community that has developed around it. As a result, it is become an immensely popular circuit board used in a huge number of tinkering projects all around the world. These tinkering projects spread across all sorts of different industries and concepts.

The goal of Arduino is to give people an easy way to understand and tinker with the fundamentals of computing and computer-based hardware without having to shell out the expensive costs that come with normal computing.

The Structure of an Arduino

Arduino is massively extensible, and there are a number of different hardware modules that can be used with your Arduino board. These peripherals attach to the Arduino and send data to and from the Arduino through what are called pins. There are two kinds of pins: digital and analog.

These are controlled through programs which run on the Arduino. These programs are called sketches. While Arduino programs can be written in many different languages, this book, in particular, focuses on the most common language for writing Arduino code - C.

C is a very popular programming language historically, and it is also incredible for pulling off the very specific hardware requirements that the Arduino presents. The Arduino by nature doesn't have a whole lot of processing power, so it is important that there's a language that is close enough to the hardware level that it can really easily work with data on the very low level that the Arduino demands, since the Arduino needs programs that don't use much processing power or memory at all.

Through the modules and accessories that one may connect to an Arduino, one is able to do a number of different things. This is why Arduino is a tinkerer's dream; you can do a whole lot for a very low price.

Foundations of C Programming

In order to work with Arduino properly, you need to have a bit of an idea about programming in C. As I said, we aren't going to spend a terribly long time going over everything in this chapter, but there are a number of essentials that it is important we cover for posterity's sake. We're going to talk about the basic concepts which build up programming in C so that you can work with it with immense ease and feel somewhat natural when you're finding your way around programming in Arduino.

Working with Variables and Values

Values are, to a computer, anything that mathematical operations can be performed upon. If you're familiar at all with computers, then you'll be aware that this refers to pretty much everything on a computer. Everything on a computer comes down to working with variables and values.

Values refer to anything that is ultimately parsed by a computer mathematically or that can be parsed by a computer mathematically. These are text characters, numbers, or things that the computer natively understands like binary. All of these things are values because they represent, ultimately, a mathematical value to the computer.

These values have types that refer to the value of the data before it is processed as raw data that the computer's hardware can work with. Some types are going to be used a lot more than others in Arduino programming because Arduino programming is all about efficiency. Nevertheless, we're going to spend a bit of time going over all of the types so that you have a firm and solid idea of what these types are as well as how to use them effectively.

Byte - This represents an integer value anywhere from 0 to 255. This only takes up 1 byte of data and can be especially useful in Arduino programming since so many things in Arduino programming are on a sequence of 0 to 255 anyway.

Int - This represents an integer value of the average size, roughly four bytes. It can hold relatively large values but be careful because if you get into the two million area, you're going to find yourself going far over the buffer limit for integer variables, which means that they're going to be restarting from the very lowest number that an integer can hold.

Float - This represents a floating-point number or a decimal. These aren't terribly common in Arduino programming, but they are more common than doubles. These can hold roughly up to 5 decimal places and be as large as about 32,000.

Double - This represents a double-precision floating point number. These are twice the size of floating-point numbers in terms of system memory, but they are far more accurate than normal floats and can have a larger non-decimal number than floating points do.

Unsigned values - These are the same size as their normal values, like unsigned ints and floats, but they don't have the capacity for negative numbers. This means that they start at 0 and can store positive numbers twice as big as normal integers and floats can, but at the price of not being able to store any negative numbers. When you're working with non-negative numbers, these are a great place to start.

Short - These are integer values that are half the size of integer values but twice the size of byte values. They can hold numbers into the 30,000s, but not any bigger than that. If you're working with smaller numbers, you'll probably want to use these over integers just because they use up less memory.

Long - These are integer values that are twice the size of normal integers, which means they can hold numbers well into the two billion areas, but there is no default value type large enough for any number bigger than that aside from unsigned longs which can be roughly four and a half billion.

Char - These represent ASCII character values. These are essentially any symbols that can be parsed by a computer and generally are used in order to store and print characters. Characters can be anything from the symbolic representation of a number, like '7', or an alphabetical character like 'a,' or a symbol like '?'. Essentially, if your computer can print it, it is probably a character.

With that, we've covered all of the major data types available for you to use in C and Arduino. There are more, don't misunderstand, but these are the primary ones that you need to understand for right now.

Assignment and Math

Assigning a value to a variable is really easy. You do so with the assignment operator: =. Like so:

int myVariable = 6;

You can also manipulate variables in this same way.

myVariable = 7;

You can perform math operations in order to create new values. You do this by using the mathematical operators, also known as arithmetic operators. The arithmetic operators in C are like so:

b + c

This signifies addition, of course.

b - c

This signifies subtraction.

b * c

This signifies multiplication.

b / c

This signifies division.

b % c

This signifies the modulo. The modulo is the remainder of a given division problem. For example, 5 % 2 would be 1, since 5 / 2 = 2 with a remainder of 1.

There are also some shorthand assignment operators. You can change the value of a single variable by adding an equal's sign to any of the above operators, like so:

a += 1

This would be the same as "a = a + 1". The meaning is consistent across all of the other symbols.

a += 1 and a -= 1 have shorthand forms themselves in a++ or a--. ++ and -- indicate that we're going to either increase the variable by one or decrease it by one, respectively.

With that, we've covered the mathematical operators of C and are ready to move on to other concepts.

Arrays

Sometimes, you need to store multiple values at once. We'll be talking more about arrays more when we start to talk about strings, but for right now, we can cover the bare essentials of arrays. We already covered them in passing in the book prior, so we aren't really looking to establish an encyclopedic knowledge of them right now, anyway. Regardless, we are going to cover them enough such that you have a refresher on them.

So, what are arrays? Arrays offer a way for you to essentially group values together by a common idea. As we have established, values are stored at random places in the computer's memory. They are then accessed in the memory whenever they're needed. Arrays serve two purposes in this arena, then.

First, they tell the computer "hey, these things are alike, and they're going to be referenced at about the same time pretty often, so we should be putting them near each other so that way the total time to get from one to another is lesser."

Then, as a result of that, they tell the computer that the values should be near one another in the computer's memory. This ensures that there is minimal travel and retrieval time from one value to the next in the computer's memory. It also enables us to perform operations that we wouldn't normally, like working through the pieces of data in memory in a procedural way as we'll talk about here in a bit.

Arrays essentially set up a contiguous or connected, areas of memory that is the size of n elements of the array times the s size of a data type. So, if a data type takes up 4 bytes of memory, and the array has four elements, it clears out and allocates 16 bytes worth of memory right next to each other.

These can then be assigned values individually according to the data type of the array. So, if you created an integer array, you could assign integers to the elements in that array.

You can declare an array like so:

dataType arrayName[size];

You can also populate it (or partially populate it, at least) by including values in brackets after your declaration of the array.

int myArray[3] = {0, 2, 7};

The indices of an array start counting at 0. You refer to a given element of an array by referring to its index. So, if you wanted to refer to the second element of an array, you'd do it like so:

myArray[1];

// this would be 2, since 2 is the element at index 1, which is position 2, within the array.

You can see that arrays are actually relatively easy to understand, but they're nonetheless a fundamental concept for you to work with and try to ingrain as much as possible if you want to be a good Arduino programmer. You're going to inevitably come upon this concept quite a bit in your time programming Arduino sketches, so you need to know it.

Truth and Logic

It is now time that we rehash a concept that we perhaps didn't go into as much detail on as we should have in the book prior: truth and logic. These concepts are absolutely intrinsic to programming in general, not to mention intrinsic to Arduino programming, so it is important that you understand them.

So, let's start with a simple question - what is logic? Logic is ultimately the use of comparison to reach some particular end result.

However, it also has another definition: the combination of premises and conclusions in the pursuit of some sort of *truth*. Note that logic and truth are not mutually exclusive. The ideas of logic can be used as a foundation for nonsensical things. For example, if my argument were like so:

All dogs are blue

I have a dog

My dog is blue

These statements are logically sound just based on the fundamental structure of the argument. It is not, however, true because its premise of all dogs being blue is incorrect. However, this does mean that by extension that many things can be figured out in a logical manner and that we can use logic based upon truthful premises in order to figure out a truthful conclusion.

These logical premises, in the context of programming, are known as *comparisons*. Comparisons essentially take one thing and another thing and then compare them to something else in order to determine whether something is true.

For example, take 3 and 7; if I were to say that "3 is more than 7", this is a logical comparison between these two values. This entire statement would be false since 3 is not more than 7.

In programming, we can do this with any given variables and values that we want so long as they are comparable. You can even overload these operators in order to define new ways for things to be comparable when you start with C++ and similar languages.

For right now, though, let's focus on the things which allow us to compare values. These are known as *comparison operators*. The comparison operators in C and, by extension, Arduino is like so:

```
s==t
```

This checks to see whether or not s and t are equal.

```
s<t
```

This checks to see whether or not s is less than t.

```
s<=t
```

This checks to see whether or not s is less than or equal to t.

```
s>t
```

This checks to see whether or not s is more than t.

```
s>=t
```

This checks to see whether or not s is either greater than or equal to t.

```
s!=t
```

This checks to see whether or not s is *not equal* to t.

One of these comparisons has two names: a *statement* and an *expression*. In programming, they're generally referred to as *expressions* in order to not confuse them with the computer science concept of the statement, but you can actually evaluate more than one of these expressions at once. This is known as *statement calculus*, and it occurs through the use of what are called *logical operators*.

There are many logical operators, but the ones in C that you most need to know are like so:

```
A&&B
```

Checks to see if both expression A and expression B are true.

```
A||B
```

!A

Checks to see if the statement A is *not* true. If it is *not* true, then we will return true since the statement "not A" *is* true.

If you're familiar at all with discrete mathematics or symbolic logic, then you'll see quite easily how many of the concepts carry over from it. However, even if you aren't familiar, they're still very easy for you to grasp nonetheless.

Conditionals

Now that we've talked a bit about logic and truth, we can build on that knowledge to talk about what is called *conditional statements*. Conditional statements are one major part of control flow. Control flow is extremely prominent in computer science, and almost every application you've ever used will have some degree of control flow built into it. Control flow is, after all, the basic way that you can give your program some sort of "intelligence," if we're defining intelligence as the capacity to make decisions based off of given data.

These can take two forms: the passive and the active conditional. The passive conditional is the most basic form, so we're going to cover that first.

The passive conditional is called so because there is no obligation for the program to run the code of the conditional. For example, if the program gets to the conditional and the condition isn't met, the code is skipped altogether, and the program moves on to the next part of the program.

The passive conditional is established through the *if statement*. The if statement just evaluates whether or not a given condition is true and then will execute the code within the if statement's code block if it is true. Otherwise, the code block will be skipped entirely. The syntax for an if statement is like so:

```
if (condition) {

// code goes within

}
```

This is complemented by the *active conditional*. The active conditional is parallel to the passive conditional because it forces the program to execute *some* code even if the statement isn't true. So in essence, if the statement is true, then the code within *that* code block will run. Otherwise, an alternative code block that has been written will be executed. This is done through the *else* statement.

```
if (condition) {

// code goes within

} else {

// back-up code is here

}
```

However, you may realize that sometimes you want to test more than one condition. You can do this with the *else if* statement which is supposed to be sandwiched between your if and else statements. You can supply additional conditions to be tested if the initial condition tested doesn't turn out to be true. It will test conditions in sequence, and if none of them are true, then the else statement will execute. The syntax for an if statement is like so:

```
if (condition) {

} else if (condition) {

} else if (condition) {

} else {

}
```

With as many or as few else if statements as you really want there to be. There is no upward or downward bound so don't worry too much about that.

Loops

Loops are an essential part of programming. In the first book we only really covered for loops, but in this book, we're going to cover both for loops and while loops. Loop logic is an essential part of our daily lives, but a lot of the time we fail to consider how important it really is to things that we do every single day.

For example, consider the act of counting from 1 to 5. You start at the number one; you say the number out loud by forming your mouth into the proper shape and expelling air, then you add 1 to the number; this repeats until you reach the number 6. At the number 6, you see that we are now bigger than the number 5 so you no longer say the number aloud.

This is a relatively simple example, but it is an important one nonetheless because it really frames just how insidious and important loop logic is.

There are two different main forms of loops in C that you'll need to know: for loops and while loops. We're going to cover while loops first because they're far simpler in concept.

While loops are relatively simple to understand but they're harder to know when to use accurately. Much of the time, you're going to be using for loops just because they seem to have more obvious and immediate uses than while loops do.

With for loops, you have really obvious bounds, but with while loops, you don't. For this reason, while loops are best suited to those cases where you don't have an actual finite number of times for a loop to run.

A while loop simply checks a condition and then runs the code within the body of the loop for as long as that condition is met. If that condition is ever not met, then the loop will exit. Easy enough!

The syntax for a while loop is like so:

while (condition) {

//loop's internal code

}

While loops are best suited to the concept of the "game loop." These loops aren't exclusive to games, of course; they just express the idea of a game, because games will do the same thing over and over until a win or lose condition is met. When those conditions are met, the game is considered over.

The game loop is based on the idea of having either a true or false variable that is changed to the opposite when a certain condition is met. So, for example, the code may be:

#define TRUE 1

#define FALSE 0

int bHasWon = FALSE;

while (bHasWon == FALSE) {

// code goes here

}

Then have something that will change bHasWon to TRUE when the player wins. This will indicate that the loop should be terminated because the win condition has been met. Of course, this logic - again - can be used for many things aside from games. Anything with a central main menu will in fact likely use this sort of loop logic.

The other kind of loop is the *for* loop. The primary purpose of the for loop is to allow you to iterate through a given set of data with ease. For loops start with the creation of an iterator variable, which can be named whatever you want. The iteration step can be many things, but it normally is by 1 (*iterator++* or *iterator--* for +1 or -1 each time, respectively).

The syntax for a for loop is like so:

for (iterator declaration; condition; iteration step) {

// code goes within

}

So to print out every number in an array, we could do the following:

```c
for (int i = 0; i < (sizeof(myArray)/sizeof(myArray[0]); i++)

{

printf("%s\n", myArray[i]);

}
```

Where sizeof(myArray)/sizeof(myArray[0]) gets the number of elements within the array altogether.

Functions

The last thing that we need to talk about and rehash before moving on to the next chapter is the concept of *functions*. Functions are a foundational concept in C programming and Arduino by extension. You're going to run into them a lot, so it is important that you understand exactly how they work. Fortunately, they aren't a very terribly difficult concept to understand! Functions simply are based around the idea of breaking something down into code which can be reused over and over.

Functions may be familiar to you through things like past math classes, where you would have something like f(x) = y. X was the argument, and the function manipulated x in order to give you the value y. Functions in computer science are relatively similar (and are very much similar to higher level functions in mathematics, but I'm not so willing to assume that everybody who reads this book has already worked with those, so I'm going to pull back on that one.)

Functions have a few basic parts. First, they have their declaration. In C, you either have to declare a new function at the start of the file, called prototyping, or you have to put it before your main function. For simplicity's sake, we'll go ahead and just prototype them at the start of our file and put them after our sketch's primary functions.

Functions also have a return type. This is the kind of value that they *give back* at the end of the function. So, for example, a function called *convertTemp* would probably give back a decimal number. Therefore, the type of function would be a *float* or a *double*.

Functions can also be written which *don't* have a return type. These functions are called *void* functions. They are valid, especially for performing certain operations that are to be done over and over but aren't particularly mathematical in and of themselves, like printing text to a serial or spinning a motor or something of the like.

Functions also have *arguments*. A function doesn't *have* to have arguments, but you can *give* a function an argument. A function's arguments are defined in its declaration. You can tell the types of the arguments as well as the placeholder names. You can then treat the arguments as variables within the body of the function and feed in the actual values when you call the function later in the program.

Again, though, a function doesn't necessarily *have* to have an argument. This isn't a requirement for a working function. Remember that as you go forward!

The syntax for prototyping a function is like so:

functionType functionName(arguments, if any);

And the syntax for actually writing a function is like so:

functionType functionName(arguments, if any) {

// code within the function

// return valueName if necessary;

}

So, let's make a function which will return the volume of a cone as a float. This is going to need two arguments, radius and height. It will be a double since we're working with pi and want it to be as accurate as possible. We will feed in doubles as arguments, too.

We could prototype the function near the start of our program like so:

double volumeOfCone(double radius, double height);

Then at some point in the program afterward, but not within another function, we could include the actual body of our function like so:

```
double volumeOfCone(double radius, double height) {

return 0.33333333 * 3.141569 * (radius * radius) * height;

}
```

We can then treat the return value of this function as a value of itself. So, we could create a double variable and assign the return value of this function to it:

```
double volumeOfConeRThreeHFive = volumeOfCone(3.00, 5.00);
```

This would return the volume of a cone with a radius of three and height of five and save it to the variable we created. We can also insert it anywhere that value is accepted, like in a printf statement or into a formatted string or something similar.

With that, we've covered the last thing that we needed to go back over before we get into some of the dense and meaty concepts within this book. In the chapters to follow, we're going to be going over much more in-depth programming concepts as we try to figure out the world of programming in Arduino at a greater level than we had before.

CHAPTER 16: More In-Depth Computer Science Topics

See, working with computers - especially something so precise and hardware-limited as the Arduino - can be immensely rewarding, but if you want to be good at it, you have to have a very firm understanding of a lot of underlying concepts.

It is perfectly fine, for example, to understand what variables *are*, but if you don't understand how they *work*, you may end up wasting a lot of computing power with them when you really don't mean to. And again, when you're working with something like Arduino, that's the last thing that you want to do.

So, in this chapter, we're going to be building on some of our topics that we've already discussed so that you can be an all-around better Arduino programmer and, in turn, a better C/C++ programmer. By the end of this chapter, you're going to feel as though you have a firmer grasp on a lot of different concepts.

Memory Management and Pointers

The first thing that we're going to talk about in this chapter is the concept of memory management and pointers. This is an immensely important topic, especially when we're talking about Arduino. You don't have a lot of onboard memory to work with, so you need to make the best of what you have.

This can be a little tricky for newer programmers to grasp. In fact, it is tricky enough that in the first book, you were warned to stay away from this in particular. This is because it is a relatively high-level topic. After all, the very idea of pointers gets into some pretty low-level programming that you most likely haven't had any experience with.

Let's think back to a second to our discussion about data and data types. We talked about how you could create variables and all of the things that you can do with them. One thing we didn't really talk about, however, is how these variables work in terms of the computer's memory.

Computers store variables for running the length of a process called the *random-access memory*. You can think of random-access memory as space that can be allocated dynamically and as needed in accordance with the current demands of the program. All values which are worked with by the programmer and the program are stored, to some degree, in the random-access memory. Variables can be defined, which allocate a set space of random-access memory that is the size of the defined variable.

Variables, too, by their very nature, are essentially references to the places that a value sits within the computer's memory. When you refer to a variable, though, you aren't actually working with that *value* necessarily. For example, when you pass a variable to a function, you aren't sending the variable *itself*. Instead, you're sending a *copy* of the variable's value to be manipulated by the newer function. This copy is then disposed of when the function is finished.

In the olden days of computing, this made a bit of sense. After all, you don't necessarily want to *change* the value of some variables every time that you send those to a function. It makes sense for such a case *not to* be the default. Additionally, functions are also stored in the computer's memory in a certain way such that it makes more sense to send them values directly than to send them references to values elsewhere in memory. It makes them, in a manner of speaking, run more efficiently.

However, there are certainly cases where you would want to refer to the value of a variable itself and not just to the value that the variable *refers*. For these cases, you'd want to use pointers. Note at the same time that it is certainly possible to work through most Arduino sketches without ever having to use pointers. However, there are times where you will be working with a data structure or need to *create* a data structure, and in these cases, a working knowledge of pointers is very useful.

Not to mention that whether we're talking in terms of general programming and Arduino programming specifically, pointers are something you *need* to know because they are an important concept of *memory management*. You have to understand memory management in order to write efficient programs, and you need to at the very least understand the concept - if not for Arduino then for anything else that you want to program.

So, what are the key points to take away from all of this? Well, first and foremost, what are pointers? Pointers offer a method for you to refer to a value by its place in memory rather than just by a copy of its value. This is important why? Because it allows you to pass and work with direct values rather than simply copies of those values that you may have through variables. This is foundational to programming in C and will also probably come up sometimes during Arduino programs. While generally, you can write entire sketches without ever even using pointers, it is still good knowledge to have for when you are looking through other people's sketches and learning from the code that they're writing.

So, how do pointers *work* then? Pointers work through a combination of operators called *reference* and *dereference* operators. You can use these in order to create new pointer variables and point them toward an already existing variable.

The first thing that you're going to do is create a new pointer of to the type of value that you're wanting to point. You do this by using the reference operator *. So, for example, let's say we had this:

int apples = 3;

And we wanted to create a pointer that would point to this variable. The first thing that we would do is create a new pointer:

int *ptr;

You can put the reference operator wherever. Most prefer to stick it on the variable name, but others prefer to put it with the type. Others still put it equidistant between the two with a space between both. It depends on the coding conventions of whatever you're working with, but generally putting it with the variable name is a safe bet.

Afterward, what you're going to do is define to the address you want it to point. You do this through the *dereference* operator: &. You set the pointer variable *itself* to this, not the pointer variable with the reference operator. So, like this:

int *ptr;

ptr = &apples;

Then, whenever we go and modify the ptr variable through the reference operator, it will change the *value* stored at the address that we pointed it to. Like so:

*ptr = 4;

```
printf("%d", apples);
```

// this would print out *four* since we changed the value at the address referred to by the variable *apples* to be 4 rather than 3.

You can see pretty plainly how this would have a lot of utility to you as a programmer when you're trying to pass variables between functions and work with variables in a complex manner. Being able to directly manipulate pointers like this has a lot of useful perks, too. When you're working with a platform where memory is both as limited and as crucial as the Arduino, you're going to want to have at least the *ability* to work with memory directly. There are some more essential things that you will want to, but they are an advanced topic and aren't within the scope of this book. They also aren't particularly useful to Arduino programming itself, such as direct memory allocation through the *malloc* function.

Regardless, knowing how to work with pointers will push you forward as an Arduino programmer because when you do encounter pointers in the wild or have to create functions that pass variables that need to be directly modified, you can do so with ease and not be pulling your hair out in confusion.

Stacks

Stacks are yet another extremely important computer science concept. They're important primarily because they work in a really crucial and integral way with things like pointers and arrays. So, what are they?

This is a bit more in-depth than Arduino but, you will still inevitably run into the basic stack terminology in discussions on Arduino programming, so it is important that you have a solid idea of what the stack is and how it can be used.

"Stack" is actually a relatively versatile term. The idea of a "stack" simply refers to what it sounds like - a stack of values. You can add variables to this stack. Imagine a block tower. This is essentially how a stack works.

You can put things on top of the stack, and these things are also the first things to be *removed* from the stack. This is especially useful in algorithmic programming, but it does bear some use in Arduino programming as well. Why? Because when you're dealing with complex and limited memory structures, you're going to inevitably run into many occasions where the best path forward is to use a stack. This is because the stack is very memory-easy. It doesn't demand anything aside from the location of the last thing in the stack and the current thing in the stack, and these things are easy to use.

It also gives you an incredibly easy way to refer back to data that you've already used, so that's pretty nifty in and of itself. Stacks are, in essence, an extremely useful tool for any programmer, and there are some Arduino IDE functions that actually reference the concept of a stack and build on the concept.

The stack is built of two essential functions: pushing and popping. Both are extremely easy to understand, so we shouldn't need to spend too much time going over what they actually are.

Pushing refers to adding something *to* the stack. It is a pretty straightforward concept. You can push a value onto the stack in order to save it for later and instantly recall it without having to worry about things such as the *name* of the variable on top of the stack or its value.

Popping refers to taking something *off* of the stack. When you pop a value from a stack, you remove the thing that was most recently added to the stack and take its value. You can then use its value however you like. If you want to return the value to the stack, just remember that you're going to have to *push* it on there again. When you pop something from the stack and remove it, the second-to-last thing that was pushed is now the first thing to be popped.

Again, the stack is a relatively simple concept, but it is nonetheless incredibly important to the overall idea of computer science as well as building and expanding your horizons in order to be better programming in general.

Structures

One of the nuances of Arduino programming and C in general that a lot of people don't take the time to learn as a newer programmer is the idea of *structures*. Structures are a relatively well-kept secret, but they can be incredibly useful.

Perhaps you've heard the term *object-oriented programming*. Structures in C were in many ways' precursors to the idea of object-oriented programming. While they aren't able to be anywhere near as extensively programmed as object-oriented concepts are able to be, they do offer a brilliant way for a programmer to group certain ideas together into a singular structure.

So, what exactly is a structure? Providing some definition for it will help you to get a better idea of how you can use it. Many times, there are concepts in programming that would make a lot more sense if you were to bundle them by putting them together. A great example is to think of a cat. You may need to work with several different *ideas* of a cat in your program, and for that, you'd be defining all sorts of different variables even though they all have a bunch of features in common. So, instead of doing this:

cat1Legs = 4;

cat2Legs = 4;

cat3Legs = 4;

cat1Color = 'brown';

cat2Color = 'black';

cat3Color = 'white with black spots';

cat1Breed = 'tabby';

cat2Breed = 'persian';

cat3Breed = 'american shorthair';

You can just define all of these in a single way and then work with them at a later point by accessing their *member data*. You do this through the use of a period. The syntax for defining a structure in C is like so:

struct NameOfStruct {

// data within struct

};

So, using the cat example:

```
struct MyCat {

int numberOfLegs;

String color;

String breed;

};
```

You could then define cats like so:

```
MyCat cat1 = {4, 'brown', 'tabby'};

MyCat cat2 = {4, 'black', 'persian'};

MyCat cat3 = {4, 'white with black spots', 'american shorthair'};
```

You can see how this presents the programmer with a much easier way to group important data together. There's a good chance you aren't going to be using this data *super* often, but it does allow you to have such a way to *do* this. It is important that you know what it is because you will eventually see it.

All of these concepts are important to Arduino because Arduino is far more restricted in terms of memory and processing power than your home computer would be. It is important that you know how to use these concepts so that you can make the most out of your Arduino's processing ability as well as write simpler and more elegant sketches than you would have otherwise. For example, you could create a structure that held three-byte variables called r, g, and b in order to program your RGB colors alongside the same lines in a simple manner. You could define new colors doing this to access them easily later on in your program, like so:

```
struct color {

byte r, g, b;

};
```

```
color blue = {0, 0, 255};
```

See how simple that is? But the utility of doing such a thing is pretty plainly obvious!

In this chapter, we've covered three major programming concepts that you're going to inevitably come across when you're working with other people's Arduino code and learning from what they've written, so it was important that I develop your ability to parse and work with these ideas.

CHAPTER 17: Arduino API Functions

In this chapter, we're going to start going into a lot of detail on functions that are provided by the Arduino API. The first book had a lot to do with the bare fundamentals of programming. This is great and all, but we didn't really get too much experience with the Arduino API itself. Our goal now is to get some experience with the numerous functions that are provided by the Arduino interface for programmers to use.

The Arduino API is the rich set of different things that are provided to the hopeful Arduino programmer to give them more options in their programming. The Arduino team has done a fantastic job of providing a full-featured API that gives the programmer a large variety of different things that they can do within the context of their Arduino tinkering.

We're going to be dividing these by section and going into a lot more information on each function, so settle in tight. What you get from this chapter is a full reference on Arduino programming that you can swing back to whenever you need.

Digital Input and Output

There are a number of functions defined by the Arduino API in order to allow you to work with digital pins. This section is dedicated to those functions, three in particular.

pinMode(pin, INPUT - OUTPUT - or INPUT_PULLUP)

This allows you to specify a given pin and then designate whether that pin will act as an *input* or act as an *output*. Newer Arduino models are able to have pins enabled through pullup resistors using the INPUT_PULLUP mode.

Analog Input and Output

On top of the digital pins, you also have your analog pins. These functions are intended to read voltage from a given pin, always between 0 and 5 volts. The upper range will be closer to *1023* while the lower will be closer to *0*.

*analogRead(*pin)

This will read the voltage from a given pin and return it as an integer from 0 to 1023.

analogReference(type)

This will configure the voltage to be used as a reference depending upon the type of your Arduino.

Most of the time, you can specify "type" as DEFAULT or INTERNAL. There are a few cases where you'll want to specify a different reference voltage.

analogWrite(pin, value)

This will write a given voltage valued from 0 to 1023, with 1023 being 4.99999 volts and 0 being 0 volts.

Advanced Input and Output

These don't really fall under either the digital or analog categories, but they're more advanced input and output categories that will allow you to do more in general with your Arduino board.

*tone(*pin, frequency, OPTIONAL duration*)*

This allows you to specify a given frequency and then generate a square wave of that frequency on a given pin.

noTone(pin)

This will stop the tone being generated by the tone function.

pulseIn(pin, value)

This will allow you to read the pulse of a given pin. If the pin is fluctuating from high to low, then it will return the time in microseconds between the high and low. Because pulses may not be completely even, you can actually specify whether you want it to read the HIGH pulse (the time for the HIGH value to change to LOW) or the LOW pulse (the time for the LOW value to change to HIGH).

pulseInLong(pin, value)

This is just like the function before, but instead of returning an integer number of microseconds, it will return a *long* number of microseconds, which essentially offers a much larger time dimension for which you can receive data.

*shiftIn(*dataPin, clockPin, bitOrder*)*

This will send a byte's worth of data to a given pin, bit by bit. The data pin is the pin where you're going to be sending each bit, the clock pin is the pin which will designate that dataPin has read data, and the bitOrder can be either MSBFIRST or LSBFIRST (Most significant or least significant bit first, respectively.)

shiftOut(dataPin, clockPin, bitOrder, value)

This is much like the function before, but it allows you to *send* data to a pin one bit at a time. Everything else is the same, but you can send out data using the *value* argument. The value argument must be of the type *byte*.

Time

These functions are intended to help you in working with time-sensitive things in the Arduino scope.

delay(value)

This allows you to pause your sketch for a certain amount of time specified by the integer *value* in milliseconds.

delayMicroseconds(value)

This is functionally the same as the delay() function except for the fact that it uses microseconds instead of milliseconds.

Math

Believe it or not, programming sometimes involves a lot of math. The math functions in the Arduino API are similar in many ways to those math functions defined by the C math library, but they keep you from having to import any additional mathematical libraries. Even if you don't use much math in your program, you'll still benefit from knowing that these exist because you never know when you might need them.

abs(value)

This function returns the absolute value of a given number or the distance between zero and a given number on a number line.

constrain(variant, lowerBound, upperBound)

This allows you to create a function such that a number will always be within the lower and upper bound.

map(number, fromMin, fromMax, toMin, toMax)

This will map a number from one range to another range.

max(number1, number2)

Will return the highest number of number1 or number2. Simple enough!

min(number1, number2)

Pretty much the exact opposite of the max function. This will return the lowest of the two numbers.

pow(base, exponent)

This will allow you to take a given number and then raise it to an exponent. C, which doesn't have a built in exponential operator, makes great use of this function.

sq(number)

This will return the square of a given number. A shorthand for *pow(number, 2)*.

sqrt(number)

This will calculate the square root of a given number.

cos(angle)

This will compute the cosine of a given angle, with the angle to be specified in radians.

sin(angle)

This will compute the sin of a given angle, with the angle to be specified in radians.

tan(angle)

This will compute the tangent of a given angle, with the angle to be specified in radians.

Characters

While they will be rare, it is important that you have a set of functions primed for you to use whenever you're working with character sets.

isAlpha(character)

This will return whether or not the character is alphabetical.

isAlphaNumeric(character)

This will return whether or not the character is either alphabetic or numeric.

isAscii()

This will return whether or not the character is an ASCII character.

isControl()

This will return whether or not a character is a control character.

isDigit()

This will return whether or not a character is a number.

isGraph()

This will return whether or not the character is something that has visual data. A space, for example, does not have visual data.

isHexadecimalDigit()

This will return whether or not the character is hexadecimal.

isLowerCase()

This will return whether or not the character is lowercase.

isPrinable()

This will return whether or not the character can be printed to the console.

isPunct()

This will return whether or not the character is a punctuation mark.

isSpace()

This will return whether or not the character is a space.

isUpperCase()

This will return whether or not the character is in upper case.

isWhiteSpace()

This will return whether or not the character is a whitespace character, like a tab, space, or line break.

Random Numbers

These functions will allow you to create random numbers in your program. Note that computers can never be truly random and spontaneous; all things are based on inputs, and nothing will ever be without these inputs in a computer. As a result, the random function *must* be seeded.

randomSeed(number)

This starts the random number generator. You feed a number in, and it starts at some random point within the sequence of the pseudo-random number generator's numerical sequence.

random(OPTIONAL minimum, maximum)

This will act as the bounds to your random number generation. The maximum value is the highest random number that you will allow, and the minimum input is the lowest value you will allow. If you don't specify a minimum, then the minimum will be assumed to be 0.

Bitwise Functions

These functions allow you to work with bits and bytes, which are the smallest pieces of data that a computer will work with. You can, theoretically, work with smaller values (in terms of overall computing power required), but these are the smallest practical values that you're going to work with while programming for Arduino.

bit(bitNum)

This will return the value of a given bit.

bitClear(variable, bit)

This will set the given *bit* of a specified numeric *variable* to 0.

bitRead(variable, bit)

This will give back the *bit* of a specified numeric *variable*.

bitSet(variable, bit)

This will set a given *variable's bit* as position denoted by *bit* to 1.

bitWrite(variable, bit, 0 or 1)

This will set the *bit* at the given position within the *variable* to either 0 or 1, depending on what you say.

highByte(value)

This will return the highest byte of a given value.

lowByte(value)

This will return the *lowest* byte of a given value.

CHAPTER 18: Using the Stream class (And Working with Strings)

This deserved its own chapter. While this also deals heavily with using the Arduino API in an effective manner, this is such a broad lesson that we really needed to break it into its own chapter so that we could properly

discuss it.

The stream class is a relatively simple concept to grasp. The stream class in itself is based on using reading information from a certain source and using this within your sketch. Because the stream is about reading data, it is necessary that we also talk about working with the keyboard and mouse in this chapter even though these aren't related *intrinsically* to the stream class.

When you're working with data, especially reading in data, you're going to inevitably find times that you're going to need to work with sets of characters like words or sentences or anything of that nature. The idea of *strings* presents you the opportunity to do this.

Strings are basically just sets of character values that are linked together as an array. Therefore, they're contiguous in memory, and the computer sees them as one large and interconnected unit. Working with strings means learning to manipulate these units to the best of your ability.

It is really simple in and of itself. Strings are essentially just *character arrays*. This means that we're technically working with what are called *C-style Strings*, which are basically strings that have a very low level of abstraction. For example, in a lot of more modern and higher-level languages, strings aren't revealed in their character as a character array; they're rather treated as a more abstract object, even if they *are* a character array at their core.

A string is composed of the *n+1* characters, where *n* is the number of letters within the string in a general sense. So, for example, the size of a string for the word "hello" would be *six* characters. The reason it is n+1 is that the string ends in a null terminating character, \0, which indicates that the end of the array has been reached and properly terminates it.

You can define a string in the same way that you would an array. You can also make them bigger than the string that they're going to contain. When you define an array, you may give it a value right off the bat, but you can also just define their size and expand them at a later point. This also makes strings, in one manner or another, dynamic and able to be changed at a later point in the program by rewriting the data within the string.

This information is of great use to you as a programmer because strings are a fundamental part of any sort of program that handles information, especially those which handle file input and output.

We've already spent a bit of time rehashing information from the book prior, but just for the sake of clarity, we're going to go ahead and define a string:

```
char myString[6] = "hello";
```

You can then refer to this entire string at a later point by the name of the character. Most of the data that is worked with by the Arduino will be worked with in terms of bytes, and most actual textual data will be worked with in terms of C strings because characters are tremendously easy to parse.

It is important that we cover all of this so that we can actually develop an idea of how to treat strings in the context of Arduino programming alongside everything that we're going to be working on through this book.

Serial

While you can't necessarily implement the stream class itself, you can implement its *derivatives*, and this is where you start to find a whole lot of utility. The serial class is an extension of the stream class that allows the Arduino board to communicate with other devices such as a computer.

Serial is enacted through both the Serial port on the Arduino as well as the USB link to the computer. In this section, we're going to be outlining all of the different functions which make up the Serial class so that you can make the absolute most of this invaluable resource.

if(Serial)

Serial.begin(rate)

You're already familiar with this function. It allows you to start the serial transmission of data. You can specify the specific rate of data transmission in bits per second.

Serial.end()

This allows you to end serial communication. You can later restart the serial communication by calling the Serial.begin() function if you wish. While the serial communication is disabled, you can use the serial pins for generalized entry and exit of data.

Serial.find(string)

This will search for the given string within the data provided by the Serial. If the string is found, the method will return true. If the string is not found, the method will return false.

Serial.findUntil(string, OPTIONAL endString)

This will look for the string within the serial buffer until either the string is found or a specified terminating string is found. If the target string is found, then the method will return true. If the terminating string is found or if the method times out, it will return false.

Serial.flush()

This will allow you to halt processes until all data being sent to the serial has been sent. Straightforward!

Serial.parseFloat()

This will return the first floating point number to be provided by the serial stream. It will be brought to an end by any character that isn't a floating point.

Serial.parseInt()

This will return the first integer number to be provided by the serial stream. It will be brought to an end by the first character that isn't a digit.

Serial.peek()

This will return the very next character to be imported by the serial buffer. However, it will not remove the character from the buffer. This makes it fundamentally different from the Serial.read() method we'll be getting to momentarily. This means that you can simply see what character is coming next.

Serial.print(value, OPTIONAL format)

You can specify the format, optionally. Otherwise, integers will print as decimals by default; floats will print to two decimal places by default, and so forth.

You can send characters or strings as is to the print statement and it will print them without any issue.

Serial.println(value, OPTIONAL format)

This will allow you to print out values just like you would with the normal print method

Serial.read()

This will read in the data which is coming in through the serial port. Simple enough! It is added to an incoming stream of serial data called the serial buffer. When you read from this buffer, the information is destroyed, so be sure to save the data to a variable if you need to reuse it at some point.

Serial.readBytes(serialBuffer, numberOfBytes)

This will read in characters from the serial port to a buffer. You can determine the number of bytes that are to be read. Your buffer must be either a char array or a byte array.

Serial.readBytesUntil(terminatorCharacter, serialBuffer, numberOfBytes)

This will read in characters from the serial either until the given number of bytes has been read or until a given terminating character has been read. In either case, the method will terminate.

Serial.write()

This will write data to the serial port; however, this particular method only sends binary data to the serial port. If you need to send ASCII data, you should use the print method instead.

Serial.serialEvent()

Whenever data comes to be available for use by the serial port, this function will be called. You can then use the Serial.read() function in order to read in data from the serial port.

With that, we've covered a lot of the particular functions related to the serial class and how it pertains to programming with the Arduino API. The next thing that we're going to need to work with is the Ethernet class.

User Defined Functions

One of the ways you can help keep your code neat, organized, and modular (reusable) is to use functions in your code. Additionally, they help make your code smaller by making certain sections reusable. Functions are like tools that were created to serve a particular function, as the name suggests.

While we have already encountered a few user-defined functions, we will cover them in greater detail now and explain some of the features we may have glossed over when we encountered them last time. Let's look at the declaration of a function now:

```
float employeeEarnings (float hoursWorked, float payRate) {

float result;// this will be the value we return when this function is called. It should match the datatype before our function name.

result = hoursWorked * payRate

return result// return tells the function to send a value back once to where it was called

}
```

This function clearly takes two arguments, hoursWorked, and payRate, both of which are 'floats.' It does some simple math on them and then returns a float as a value. Return means to terminate the function and send back whatever value is placed after the word return, usually a variable, as the result of some calculations.

Let's see us call this function now to get an employee's earnings:

```
void loop () {

float hoursWorked = 37.5;

float payRate = 18.50;

float result = employeeEarnings (hoursWorked, payRate)

// result will be 693.75
```

First, the function must be declared outside of any other functions. This means you need to write the code for the function you are creating outside of either setup() or loop(), or any other user-defined function.

Let's see another example that sample sketch that could be used to smooth sensor readings:

```
int sensorSmoothing (analogPin) {

int sensorValue = 0;

for (int index = 0; index < 5, index++)

digitalWrite(LED_BUILTIN, HIGH); //Turn on LED for smoothing

sensorValue = sensorValue + analogRead(analogPin)

delay(100)// 100 millisecond delay between samples

}

digitalWrite(LED_BUILTIN, LOW);//turn off LED

sensorValue = sensorValue / 5//average the values over five samples

return sensorValue;

}
```

This kind of function can be used for smoothing the data input of many sensors if they are prone to jittery inputs. This will average the samples to give a more consistent flow of data. You can see that this code is very similar to our last example:

```
void loop () {

int sensorPin = 0;// analog pin 0

int sensorValue = sensorSmoothing (sensorPin);

}
```

Here, when we try to initialize our sensorValue variable it will call the sensorSmoothing() function on analog pin 0, and return the average result over five samples)

Functions do not always need to have parameters or return variables either. Sometimes functions can return no value and have no parameters. All they do is execute a few lines of code and then terminate bringing the compiler back to place in the code they were called.

Conclusion

The next step is to get out there and start making your own sketches! Go to your local hobby store to get some ideas or go to the community to see what new projects you might want to try. After you have an idea where you might want to go next, (robots are pretty fun!) join the community! Seriously, it is a lot of fun to build projects with friends and compare them with each other. If you feel like you don't know where to start, don't worry! There are many online sources that share coding and techniques to improve your game. Many online sites also have forums specifically tailored to helping people like you learn and show off what they have done. It is also a fantastic way to learn and grow as a hobbyist.

If you want to get started but are feeling strapped for cash, there are options. Like we've said above, there are fairly cheap modules for purchase on the Arduino site and others. Also, cheaper programming languages are available, and some are even free. Learning these languages are actually easier than you would think. If you know one programming language, the rest are easier to understand and write. There are also books at your local library that will help you learn how to code. Many libraries offer interlibrary loans, which means that you can learn about programming from books from all around you! Best of all, learning from a book from the library is absolutely free! If you have any questions about this, remember that you can go online and find others who have worked with Arduino and know how to get you started.

Arduino board can be programmed to light or fade a LED etc. The syntax used in Arduino programming is similar to C++. If you are good at C++, then programming in Arduino will be easy for you. The variables in Arduino are initialized within the setup() function. The loop() section has the block to be run repeatedly. When working with Arduino pins, you must specify the pin you need to work with. The pins are normally identified with numbers as each has a unique number. After getting the board, you have to setup Arduino IDE on your computer. This is where you will be writing your Arduino code before uploading bit to the board. Arduino code is commonly known as a sketch. You must get a source of power. However, some board types must be configured to allow power to be drawn from a computer. The effect of a sketch on the board will be seen after uploading it to the board, in which one has to click the Upload button.

There are many sensors and additions to each Arduino, so make sure you check out which you would like to employ. The great part of owning an Arduino is that you'll get the chance to try many experiments. You're not just limited to what the sensors can read, either. Come up with some ways on your own to make the machines work for you. Try programming simple requests first—like setting up blinking lights or figuring out how Arduino can monitor inputs—and see what you can do from there. I have included many Arduino codes for you to use, but feel free to find some of your own! There are many guides for help.

You can also check out some more advanced concepts we didn't have a chance to touch on here such as headers, classes, changing the clock speed for the chip, adding cores, adding libraries, there is so much that you can do with this chip, it really is incredible. Pick a direction that interests you and see where it takes you. I hope that this guide has offered you some small inspiration to go out there and try new things and see what your sketch designing skills are capable of.

Finally, thank you for finishing this book! Arduinos are a fun way to get started on your programming journey. Since you've purchased this book, we hope you've grown, and if you found this book useful in any way, a review on Amazon is always appreciated!

References

Arduino Reference. (2023). Retrieved from
https://www.arduino.cc/reference/en/language/structure/comparison
-operators/lessthan/

What is an Arduino? - learn.sparkfun.com. (2023). Retrieved from
https://learn.sparkfun.com/tutorials/what-is-an-arduino/all#the-
arduino-family

www.ingramcontent.com/pod-product-compliance
Lightning Source LLC
Chambersburg PA
CBHW070832160726
48004CB00001B/347